C-1343 CAREER EXAMINATION SERIES

This is your
PASSBOOK for...

Legal Secretary

Test Preparation Study Guide
Questions & Answers

NATIONAL LEARNING CORPORATION®

COPYRIGHT NOTICE

This book is SOLELY intended for, is sold ONLY to, and its use is RESTRICTED to individual, bona fide applicants or candidates who qualify by virtue of having seriously filed applications for appropriate license, certificate, professional and/or promotional advancement, higher school matriculation, scholarship, or other legitimate requirements of education and/or governmental authorities.

This book is NOT intended for use, class instruction, tutoring, training, duplication, copying, reprinting, excerption, or adaptation, etc., by:

1) Other publishers
2) Proprietors and/or Instructors of "Coaching" and/or Preparatory Courses
3) Personnel and/or Training Divisions of commercial, industrial, and governmental organizations
4) Schools, colleges, or universities and/or their departments and staffs, including teachers and other personnel
5) Testing Agencies or Bureaus
6) Study groups which seek by the purchase of a single volume to copy and/or duplicate and/or adapt this material for use by the group as a whole without having purchased individual volumes for each of the members of the group
7) Et al.

Such persons would be in violation of appropriate Federal and State statutes.

PROVISION OF LICENSING AGREEMENTS – Recognized educational, commercial, industrial, and governmental institutions and organizations, and others legitimately engaged in educational pursuits, including training, testing, and measurement activities, may address request for a licensing agreement to the copyright owners, who will determine whether, and under what conditions, including fees and charges, the materials in this book may be used them. In other words, a licensing facility exists for the legitimate use of the material in this book on other than an individual basis. However, it is asseverated and affirmed here that the material in this book CANNOT be used without the receipt of the express permission of such a licensing agreement from the Publishers. Inquiries re licensing should be addressed to the company, attention rights and permissions department.

All rights reserved, including the right of reproduction in whole or in part, in any form or by any means, electronic or mechanical, including photocopying, recording, or by any information storage and retrieval system, without permission in writing from the Publisher.

Copyright © 2024 by
National Learning Corporation

212 Michael Drive, Syosset, NY 11791
(516) 921-8888 • www.passbooks.com
E-mail: info@passbooks.com

PUBLISHED IN THE UNITED STATES OF AMERICA

PASSBOOK® SERIES

THE *PASSBOOK® SERIES* has been created to prepare applicants and candidates for the ultimate academic battlefield – the examination room.

At some time in our lives, each and every one of us may be required to take an examination – for validation, matriculation, admission, qualification, registration, certification, or licensure.

Based on the assumption that every applicant or candidate has met the basic formal educational standards, has taken the required number of courses, and read the necessary texts, the *PASSBOOK® SERIES* furnishes the one special preparation which may assure passing with confidence, instead of failing with insecurity. Examination questions – together with answers – are furnished as the basic vehicle for study so that the mysteries of the examination and its compounding difficulties may be eliminated or diminished by a sure method.

This book is meant to help you pass your examination provided that you qualify and are serious in your objective.

The entire field is reviewed through the huge store of content information which is succinctly presented through a provocative and challenging approach – the question-and-answer method.

A climate of success is established by furnishing the correct answers at the end of each test.

You soon learn to recognize types of questions, forms of questions, and patterns of questioning. You may even begin to anticipate expected outcomes.

You perceive that many questions are repeated or adapted so that you can gain acute insights, which may enable you to score many sure points.

You learn how to confront new questions, or types of questions, and to attack them confidently and work out the correct answers.

You note objectives and emphases, and recognize pitfalls and dangers, so that you may make positive educational adjustments.

Moreover, you are kept fully informed in relation to new concepts, methods, practices, and directions in the field.

You discover that you are actually taking the examination all the time: you are preparing for the examination by "taking" an examination, not by reading extraneous and/or supererogatory textbooks.

In short, this PASSBOOK®, used directedly, should be an important factor in helping you to pass your test.

LEGAL SECRETARY

DUTIES:
Under general supervision, incumbents of this class perform executive legal secretarial, clerical and administrative duties for upper level administrators or professional persons, to support the efficient operation of the Law Department or District Attorney's Office. Work includes the preparation and storing of legal documents and correspondence, requiring knowledge of legal terminology and the operation of computers and word processing software. Supervision is not a responsibility of this position, but incumbents may act as a lead worker for the completion of assigned projects. Does related work as required.

EXAMPLES OF TYPICAL TASKS:
Takes and transcribes dictation of briefs, affidavits, affirmations, orders, certificates, notices, memoranda of law, letters and general memoranda. Relieves superior of administrative and office detail. Types legal documents, memoranda, reports, etc. Screens messages and telephone calls for superior. Indexes and files documents, letters and a variety of legal papers. Supervises employees of subordinate rank in the performance of secretarial and clerical tasks.

SUBJECT OF EXAMINATION:
The written test is designed to evaluate knowledge, skills and /or abilities in the following areas:
1. **Grammar/Usage/Punctuation** - The grammar and usage questions test for the ability to apply the basic rules of grammar and usage. The punctuation questions test for a knowledge of the correct placement of punctuation marks in sentences. You will be presented with sets of four sentences from each of which you must choose the sentence that contains a grammatical, usage, or punctuation error.
2. **Keyboarding practices** - These questions test for a knowledge of preferred practices in such areas as letter format, capitalization, hyphenation, plurals, possessives, word division, word and figure style for numbers, and common proofreading marks. In addition, there will be a passage to proofread followed by questions on how to correct the errors in the passage.
3. **Legal terminology documents and forms** - These questions test for the ability to recognize definitions of specific common legal terms or the term which fits a certain description. The questions are presented in various forms such as simple definitions, examples of terminology, and the use of this terminology within documents and forms related to the legal field.
4. **Office practices** - These questions test for a knowledge of generally agreed-upon practices governing the handling of situations which typists, stenographers, secretaries, and office assistants encounter in their work, as well as a knowledge of efficient and effective methods used to accomplish office tasks. The questions cover such topics as planning work flow; setting priorities; dealing effectively with staff, visitors, and callers; filing and retrieving information; safeguarding confidentiality; using office equipment; and making procedural decisions and recommendations which contribute to a well-managed office.
5. **Office record keeping** - These questions test your ability to perform common office record keeping tasks. The test consists of two or more "sets" of questions, each set concerning a different problem. Typical record keeping problems might involve the organization or collation of data from several sources; scheduling; maintaining a record system using running balances; or completion of a table summarizing data using totals, subtotals, averages and percents.
6. **Spelling** - These questions test for the ability to spell words that are used in written business communications.

HOW TO TAKE A TEST

I. YOU MUST PASS AN EXAMINATION

A. *WHAT EVERY CANDIDATE SHOULD KNOW*

Examination applicants often ask us for help in preparing for the written test. What can I study in advance? What kinds of questions will be asked? How will the test be given? How will the papers be graded?

As an applicant for a civil service examination, you may be wondering about some of these things. Our purpose here is to suggest effective methods of advance study and to describe civil service examinations.

Your chances for success on this examination can be increased if you know how to prepare. Those "pre-examination jitters" can be reduced if you know what to expect. You can even experience an adventure in good citizenship if you know why civil service exams are given.

B. *WHY ARE CIVIL SERVICE EXAMINATIONS GIVEN?*

Civil service examinations are important to you in two ways. As a citizen, you want public jobs filled by employees who know how to do their work. As a job seeker, you want a fair chance to compete for that job on an equal footing with other candidates. The best-known means of accomplishing this two-fold goal is the competitive examination.

Exams are widely publicized throughout the nation. They may be administered for jobs in federal, state, city, municipal, town or village governments or agencies.

Any citizen may apply, with some limitations, such as the age or residence of applicants. Your experience and education may be reviewed to see whether you meet the requirements for the particular examination. When these requirements exist, they are reasonable and applied consistently to all applicants. Thus, a competitive examination may cause you some uneasiness now, but it is your privilege and safeguard.

C. *HOW ARE CIVIL SERVICE EXAMS DEVELOPED?*

Examinations are carefully written by trained technicians who are specialists in the field known as "psychological measurement," in consultation with recognized authorities in the field of work that the test will cover. These experts recommend the subject matter areas or skills to be tested; only those knowledges or skills important to your success on the job are included. The most reliable books and source materials available are used as references. Together, the experts and technicians judge the difficulty level of the questions.

Test technicians know how to phrase questions so that the problem is clearly stated. Their ethics do not permit "trick" or "catch" questions. Questions may have been tried out on sample groups, or subjected to statistical analysis, to determine their usefulness.

Written tests are often used in combination with performance tests, ratings of training and experience, and oral interviews. All of these measures combine to form the best-known means of finding the right person for the right job.

II. HOW TO PASS THE WRITTEN TEST

A. NATURE OF THE EXAMINATION

To prepare intelligently for civil service examinations, you should know how they differ from school examinations you have taken. In school you were assigned certain definite pages to read or subjects to cover. The examination questions were quite detailed and usually emphasized memory. Civil service exams, on the other hand, try to discover your present ability to perform the duties of a position, plus your potentiality to learn these duties. In other words, a civil service exam attempts to predict how successful you will be. Questions cover such a broad area that they cannot be as minute and detailed as school exam questions.

In the public service similar kinds of work, or positions, are grouped together in one "class." This process is known as *position-classification*. All the positions in a class are paid according to the salary range for that class. One class title covers all of these positions, and they are all tested by the same examination.

B. FOUR BASIC STEPS

1) Study the announcement

How, then, can you know what subjects to study? Our best answer is: "Learn as much as possible about the class of positions for which you've applied." The exam will test the knowledge, skills and abilities needed to do the work.

Your most valuable source of information about the position you want is the official exam announcement. This announcement lists the training and experience qualifications. Check these standards and apply only if you come reasonably close to meeting them.

The brief description of the position in the examination announcement offers some clues to the subjects which will be tested. Think about the job itself. Review the duties in your mind. Can you perform them, or are there some in which you are rusty? Fill in the blank spots in your preparation.

Many jurisdictions preview the written test in the exam announcement by including a section called "Knowledge and Abilities Required," "Scope of the Examination," or some similar heading. Here you will find out specifically what fields will be tested.

2) Review your own background

Once you learn in general what the position is all about, and what you need to know to do the work, ask yourself which subjects you already know fairly well and which need improvement. You may wonder whether to concentrate on improving your strong areas or on building some background in your fields of weakness. When the announcement has specified "some knowledge" or "considerable knowledge," or has used adjectives like "beginning principles of..." or "advanced ... methods," you can get a clue as to the number and difficulty of questions to be asked in any given field. More questions, and hence broader coverage, would be included for those subjects which are more important in the work. Now weigh your strengths and weaknesses against the job requirements and prepare accordingly.

3) Determine the level of the position

Another way to tell how intensively you should prepare is to understand the level of the job for which you are applying. Is it the entering level? In other words, is this the position in which beginners in a field of work are hired? Or is it an intermediate or advanced level? Sometimes this is indicated by such words as "Junior" or "Senior" in the class title. Other jurisdictions use Roman numerals to designate the level – Clerk I, Clerk II, for example. The word "Supervisor" sometimes appears in the title. If the level is not indicated by the title, check the description of duties. Will you be working under very close supervision, or will you have responsibility for independent decisions in this work?

4) Choose appropriate study materials

Now that you know the subjects to be examined and the relative amount of each subject to be covered, you can choose suitable study materials. For beginning level jobs, or even advanced ones, if you have a pronounced weakness in some aspect of your training, read a modern, standard textbook in that field. Be sure it is up to date and has general coverage. Such books are normally available at your library, and the librarian will be glad to help you locate one. For entry-level positions, questions of appropriate difficulty are chosen – neither highly advanced questions, nor those too simple. Such questions require careful thought but not advanced training.

If the position for which you are applying is technical or advanced, you will read more advanced, specialized material. If you are already familiar with the basic principles of your field, elementary textbooks would waste your time. Concentrate on advanced textbooks and technical periodicals. Think through the concepts and review difficult problems in your field.

These are all general sources. You can get more ideas on your own initiative, following these leads. For example, training manuals and publications of the government agency which employs workers in your field can be useful, particularly for technical and professional positions. A letter or visit to the government department involved may result in more specific study suggestions, and certainly will provide you with a more definite idea of the exact nature of the position you are seeking.

III. KINDS OF TESTS

Tests are used for purposes other than measuring knowledge and ability to perform specified duties. For some positions, it is equally important to test ability to make adjustments to new situations or to profit from training. In others, basic mental abilities not dependent on information are essential. Questions which test these things may not appear as pertinent to the duties of the position as those which test for knowledge and information. Yet they are often highly important parts of a fair examination. For very general questions, it is almost impossible to help you direct your study efforts. What we can do is to point out some of the more common of these general abilities needed in public service positions and describe some typical questions.

1) General information

Broad, general information has been found useful for predicting job success in some kinds of work. This is tested in a variety of ways, from vocabulary lists to questions about current events. Basic background in some field of work, such as sociology or economics, may be sampled in a group of questions. Often these are principles which have become familiar to most persons through exposure rather than through formal training. It is difficult to advise you how to study for these questions; being alert to the world around you is our best suggestion.

2) Verbal ability

An example of an ability needed in many positions is verbal or language ability. Verbal ability is, in brief, the ability to use and understand words. Vocabulary and grammar tests are typical measures of this ability. Reading comprehension or paragraph interpretation questions are common in many kinds of civil service tests. You are given a paragraph of written material and asked to find its central meaning.

3) Numerical ability

Number skills can be tested by the familiar arithmetic problem, by checking paired lists of numbers to see which are alike and which are different, or by interpreting charts and graphs. In the latter test, a graph may be printed in the test booklet which you are asked to use as the basis for answering questions.

4) Observation

A popular test for law-enforcement positions is the observation test. A picture is shown to you for several minutes, then taken away. Questions about the picture test your ability to observe both details and larger elements.

5) Following directions

In many positions in the public service, the employee must be able to carry out written instructions dependably and accurately. You may be given a chart with several columns, each column listing a variety of information. The questions require you to carry out directions involving the information given in the chart.

6) Skills and aptitudes

Performance tests effectively measure some manual skills and aptitudes. When the skill is one in which you are trained, such as typing or shorthand, you can practice. These tests are often very much like those given in business school or high school courses. For many of the other skills and aptitudes, however, no short-time preparation can be made. Skills and abilities natural to you or that you have developed throughout your lifetime are being tested.

Many of the general questions just described provide all the data needed to answer the questions and ask you to use your reasoning ability to find the answers. Your best preparation for these tests, as well as for tests of facts and ideas, is to be at your physical and mental best. You, no doubt, have your own methods of getting into an exam-taking mood and keeping "in shape." The next section lists some ideas on this subject.

IV. KINDS OF QUESTIONS

Only rarely is the "essay" question, which you answer in narrative form, used in civil service tests. Civil service tests are usually of the short-answer type. Full instructions for answering these questions will be given to you at the examination. But in case this is your first experience with short-answer questions and separate answer sheets, here is what you need to know:

1) **Multiple-choice Questions**

Most popular of the short-answer questions is the "multiple choice" or "best answer" question. It can be used, for example, to test for factual knowledge, ability to solve problems or judgment in meeting situations found at work.

A multiple-choice question is normally one of three types—
- It can begin with an incomplete statement followed by several possible endings. You are to find the one ending which *best* completes the statement, although some of the others may not be entirely wrong.
- It can also be a complete statement in the form of a question which is answered by choosing one of the statements listed.

- It can be in the form of a problem – again you select the best answer.

Here is an example of a multiple-choice question with a discussion which should give you some clues as to the method for choosing the right answer:

When an employee has a complaint about his assignment, the action which will *best* help him overcome his difficulty is to
    A. discuss his difficulty with his coworkers
    B. take the problem to the head of the organization
    C. take the problem to the person who gave him the assignment
    D. say nothing to anyone about his complaint

In answering this question, you should study each of the choices to find which is best. Consider choice "A" – Certainly an employee may discuss his complaint with fellow employees, but no change or improvement can result, and the complaint remains unresolved. Choice "B" is a poor choice since the head of the organization probably does not know what assignment you have been given, and taking your problem to him is known as "going over the head" of the supervisor. The supervisor, or person who made the assignment, is the person who can clarify it or correct any injustice. Choice "C" is, therefore, correct. To say nothing, as in choice "D," is unwise. Supervisors have and interest in knowing the problems employees are facing, and the employee is seeking a solution to his problem.

2) True/False Questions

The "true/false" or "right/wrong" form of question is sometimes used. Here a complete statement is given. Your job is to decide whether the statement is right or wrong.

SAMPLE: A roaming cell-phone call to a nearby city costs less than a non-roaming call to a distant city.

This statement is wrong, or false, since roaming calls are more expensive.

This is not a complete list of all possible question forms, although most of the others are variations of these common types. You will always get complete directions for answering questions. Be sure you understand *how* to mark your answers – ask questions until you do.

V. RECORDING YOUR ANSWERS

Computer terminals are used more and more today for many different kinds of exams.
For an examination with very few applicants, you may be told to record your answers in the test booklet itself. Separate answer sheets are much more common. If this separate answer sheet is to be scored by machine – and this is often the case – it is highly important that you mark your answers correctly in order to get credit.
An electronic scoring machine is often used in civil service offices because of the speed with which papers can be scored. Machine-scored answer sheets must be marked with a pencil, which will be given to you. This pencil has a high graphite content which responds to the electronic scoring machine. As a matter of fact, stray dots may register as answers, so do not let your pencil rest on the answer sheet while you are pondering the correct answer. Also, if your pencil lead breaks or is otherwise defective, ask for another.

Since the answer sheet will be dropped in a slot in the scoring machine, be careful not to bend the corners or get the paper crumpled.

The answer sheet normally has five vertical columns of numbers, with 30 numbers to a column. These numbers correspond to the question numbers in your test booklet. After each number, going across the page are four or five pairs of dotted lines. These short dotted lines have small letters or numbers above them. The first two pairs may also have a "T" or "F" above the letters. This indicates that the first two pairs only are to be used if the questions are of the true-false type. If the questions are multiple choice, disregard the "T" and "F" and pay attention only to the small letters or numbers.

Answer your questions in the manner of the sample that follows:

32. The largest city in the United States is
    A. Washington, D.C.
    B. New York City
    C. Chicago
    D. Detroit
    E. San Francisco

1) Choose the answer you think is best. (New York City is the largest, so "B" is correct.)
2) Find the row of dotted lines numbered the same as the question you are answering. (Find row number 32)
3) Find the pair of dotted lines corresponding to the answer. (Find the pair of lines under the mark "B.")
4) Make a solid black mark between the dotted lines.

VI. BEFORE THE TEST

Common sense will help you find procedures to follow to get ready for an examination. Too many of us, however, overlook these sensible measures. Indeed, nervousness and fatigue have been found to be the most serious reasons why applicants fail to do their best on civil service tests. Here is a list of reminders:

- Begin your preparation early – Don't wait until the last minute to go scurrying around for books and materials or to find out what the position is all about.
- Prepare continuously – An hour a night for a week is better than an all-night cram session. This has been definitely established. What is more, a night a week for a month will return better dividends than crowding your study into a shorter period of time.
- Locate the place of the exam – You have been sent a notice telling you when and where to report for the examination. If the location is in a different town or otherwise unfamiliar to you, it would be well to inquire the best route and learn something about the building.
- Relax the night before the test – Allow your mind to rest. Do not study at all that night. Plan some mild recreation or diversion; then go to bed early and get a good night's sleep.
- Get up early enough to make a leisurely trip to the place for the test – This way unforeseen events, traffic snarls, unfamiliar buildings, etc. will not upset you.
- Dress comfortably – A written test is not a fashion show. You will be known by number and not by name, so wear something comfortable.

- Leave excess paraphernalia at home – Shopping bags and odd bundles will get in your way. You need bring only the items mentioned in the official notice you received; usually everything you need is provided. Do not bring reference books to the exam. They will only confuse those last minutes and be taken away from you when in the test room.
- Arrive somewhat ahead of time – If because of transportation schedules you must get there very early, bring a newspaper or magazine to take your mind off yourself while waiting.
- Locate the examination room – When you have found the proper room, you will be directed to the seat or part of the room where you will sit. Sometimes you are given a sheet of instructions to read while you are waiting. Do not fill out any forms until you are told to do so; just read them and be prepared.
- Relax and prepare to listen to the instructions
- If you have any physical problem that may keep you from doing your best, be sure to tell the test administrator. If you are sick or in poor health, you really cannot do your best on the exam. You can come back and take the test some other time.

VII. AT THE TEST

The day of the test is here and you have the test booklet in your hand. The temptation to get going is very strong. Caution! There is more to success than knowing the right answers. You must know how to identify your papers and understand variations in the type of short-answer question used in this particular examination. Follow these suggestions for maximum results from your efforts:

1) Cooperate with the monitor

The test administrator has a duty to create a situation in which you can be as much at ease as possible. He will give instructions, tell you when to begin, check to see that you are marking your answer sheet correctly, and so on. He is not there to guard you, although he will see that your competitors do not take unfair advantage. He wants to help you do your best.

2) Listen to all instructions

Don't jump the gun! Wait until you understand all directions. In most civil service tests you get more time than you need to answer the questions. So don't be in a hurry. Read each word of instructions until you clearly understand the meaning. Study the examples, listen to all announcements and follow directions. Ask questions if you do not understand what to do.

3) Identify your papers

Civil service exams are usually identified by number only. You will be assigned a number; you must not put your name on your test papers. Be sure to copy your number correctly. Since more than one exam may be given, copy your exact examination title.

4) Plan your time

Unless you are told that a test is a "speed" or "rate of work" test, speed itself is usually not important. Time enough to answer all the questions will be provided, but this does not mean that you have all day. An overall time limit has been set. Divide the total time (in minutes) by the number of questions to determine the approximate time you have for each question.

5) Do not linger over difficult questions

If you come across a difficult question, mark it with a paper clip (useful to have along) and come back to it when you have been through the booklet. One caution if you do this – be sure to skip a number on your answer sheet as well. Check often to be sure that you have not lost your place and that you are marking in the row numbered the same as the question you are answering.

6) Read the questions

Be sure you know what the question asks! Many capable people are unsuccessful because they failed to *read* the questions correctly.

7) Answer all questions

Unless you have been instructed that a penalty will be deducted for incorrect answers, it is better to guess than to omit a question.

8) Speed tests

It is often better NOT to guess on speed tests. It has been found that on timed tests people are tempted to spend the last few seconds before time is called in marking answers at random – without even reading them – in the hope of picking up a few extra points. To discourage this practice, the instructions may warn you that your score will be "corrected" for guessing. That is, a penalty will be applied. The incorrect answers will be deducted from the correct ones, or some other penalty formula will be used.

9) Review your answers

If you finish before time is called, go back to the questions you guessed or omitted to give them further thought. Review other answers if you have time.

10) Return your test materials

If you are ready to leave before others have finished or time is called, take ALL your materials to the monitor and leave quietly. Never take any test material with you. The monitor can discover whose papers are not complete, and taking a test booklet may be grounds for disqualification.

VIII. EXAMINATION TECHNIQUES

1) Read the general instructions carefully. These are usually printed on the first page of the exam booklet. As a rule, these instructions refer to the timing of the examination; the fact that you should not start work until the signal and must stop work at a signal, etc. If there are any *special* instructions, such as a choice of questions to be answered, make sure that you note this instruction carefully.

2) When you are ready to start work on the examination, that is as soon as the signal has been given, read the instructions to each question booklet, underline any key words or phrases, such as *least, best, outline, describe* and the like. In this way you will tend to answer as requested rather than discover on reviewing your paper that you *listed without describing*, that you selected the *worst* choice rather than the *best* choice, etc.

3) If the examination is of the objective or multiple-choice type – that is, each question will also give a series of possible answers: A, B, C or D, and you are called upon to select the best answer and write the letter next to that answer on your answer paper – it is advisable to start answering each question in turn. There may be anywhere from 50 to 100 such questions in the three or four hours allotted and you can see how much time would be taken if you read through all the questions before beginning to answer any. Furthermore, if you come across a question or group of questions which you know would be difficult to answer, it would undoubtedly affect your handling of all the other questions.

4) If the examination is of the essay type and contains but a few questions, it is a moot point as to whether you should read all the questions before starting to answer any one. Of course, if you are given a choice – say five out of seven and the like – then it is essential to read all the questions so you can eliminate the two that are most difficult. If, however, you are asked to answer all the questions, there may be danger in trying to answer the easiest one first because you may find that you will spend too much time on it. The best technique is to answer the first question, then proceed to the second, etc.

5) Time your answers. Before the exam begins, write down the time it started, then add the time allowed for the examination and write down the time it must be completed, then divide the time available somewhat as follows:
   - If 3-1/2 hours are allowed, that would be 210 minutes. If you have 80 objective-type questions, that would be an average of 2-1/2 minutes per question. Allow yourself no more than 2 minutes per question, or a total of 160 minutes, which will permit about 50 minutes to review.
   - If for the time allotment of 210 minutes there are 7 essay questions to answer, that would average about 30 minutes a question. Give yourself only 25 minutes per question so that you have about 35 minutes to review.

6) The most important instruction is to *read each question* and make sure you know what is wanted. The second most important instruction is to *time yourself properly* so that you answer every question. The third most important instruction is to *answer every question*. Guess if you have to but include something for each question. Remember that you will receive no credit for a blank and will probably receive some credit if you write something in answer to an essay question. If you guess a letter – say "B" for a multiple-choice question – you may have guessed right. If you leave a blank as an answer to a multiple-choice question, the examiners may respect your feelings but it will not add a point to your score. Some exams may penalize you for wrong answers, so in such cases *only*, you may not want to guess unless you have some basis for your answer.

7) Suggestions
   a. Objective-type questions
      1. Examine the question booklet for proper sequence of pages and questions
      2. Read all instructions carefully
      3. Skip any question which seems too difficult; return to it after all other questions have been answered
      4. Apportion your time properly; do not spend too much time on any single question or group of questions

5. Note and underline key words – *all, most, fewest, least, best, worst, same, opposite,* etc.
6. Pay particular attention to negatives
7. Note unusual option, e.g., unduly long, short, complex, different or similar in content to the body of the question
8. Observe the use of "hedging" words – *probably, may, most likely,* etc.
9. Make sure that your answer is put next to the same number as the question
10. Do not second-guess unless you have good reason to believe the second answer is definitely more correct
11. Cross out original answer if you decide another answer is more accurate; do not erase until you are ready to hand your paper in
12. Answer all questions; guess unless instructed otherwise
13. Leave time for review

b. Essay questions
 1. Read each question carefully
 2. Determine exactly what is wanted. Underline key words or phrases.
 3. Decide on outline or paragraph answer
 4. Include many different points and elements unless asked to develop any one or two points or elements
 5. Show impartiality by giving pros and cons unless directed to select one side only
 6. Make and write down any assumptions you find necessary to answer the questions
 7. Watch your English, grammar, punctuation and choice of words
 8. Time your answers; don't crowd material

8) Answering the essay question

Most essay questions can be answered by framing the specific response around several key words or ideas. Here are a few such key words or ideas:

M's: manpower, materials, methods, money, management
P's: purpose, program, policy, plan, procedure, practice, problems, pitfalls, personnel, public relations

 a. Six basic steps in handling problems:
  1. Preliminary plan and background development
  2. Collect information, data and facts
  3. Analyze and interpret information, data and facts
  4. Analyze and develop solutions as well as make recommendations
  5. Prepare report and sell recommendations
  6. Install recommendations and follow up effectiveness

 b. Pitfalls to avoid
  1. *Taking things for granted* – A statement of the situation does not necessarily imply that each of the elements is necessarily true; for example, a complaint may be invalid and biased so that all that can be taken for granted is that a complaint has been registered

2. *Considering only one side of a situation* – Wherever possible, indicate several alternatives and then point out the reasons you selected the best one
3. *Failing to indicate follow up* – Whenever your answer indicates action on your part, make certain that you will take proper follow-up action to see how successful your recommendations, procedures or actions turn out to be
4. *Taking too long in answering any single question* – Remember to time your answers properly

IX. AFTER THE TEST

Scoring procedures differ in detail among civil service jurisdictions although the general principles are the same. Whether the papers are hand-scored or graded by machine we have described, they are nearly always graded by number. That is, the person who marks the paper knows only the number – never the name – of the applicant. Not until all the papers have been graded will they be matched with names. If other tests, such as training and experience or oral interview ratings have been given, scores will be combined. Different parts of the examination usually have different weights. For example, the written test might count 60 percent of the final grade, and a rating of training and experience 40 percent. In many jurisdictions, veterans will have a certain number of points added to their grades.

After the final grade has been determined, the names are placed in grade order and an eligible list is established. There are various methods for resolving ties between those who get the same final grade – probably the most common is to place first the name of the person whose application was received first. Job offers are made from the eligible list in the order the names appear on it. You will be notified of your grade and your rank as soon as all these computations have been made. This will be done as rapidly as possible.

People who are found to meet the requirements in the announcement are called "eligibles." Their names are put on a list of eligible candidates. An eligible's chances of getting a job depend on how high he stands on this list and how fast agencies are filling jobs from the list.

When a job is to be filled from a list of eligibles, the agency asks for the names of people on the list of eligibles for that job. When the civil service commission receives this request, it sends to the agency the names of the three people highest on this list. Or, if the job to be filled has specialized requirements, the office sends the agency the names of the top three persons who meet these requirements from the general list.

The appointing officer makes a choice from among the three people whose names were sent to him. If the selected person accepts the appointment, the names of the others are put back on the list to be considered for future openings.

That is the rule in hiring from all kinds of eligible lists, whether they are for typist, carpenter, chemist, or something else. For every vacancy, the appointing officer has his choice of any one of the top three eligibles on the list. This explains why the person whose name is on top of the list sometimes does not get an appointment when some of the persons lower on the list do. If the appointing officer chooses the second or third eligible, the No. 1 eligible does not get a job at once, but stays on the list until he is appointed or the list is terminated.

X. HOW TO PASS THE INTERVIEW TEST

The examination for which you applied requires an oral interview test. You have already taken the written test and you are now being called for the interview test – the final part of the formal examination.

You may think that it is not possible to prepare for an interview test and that there are no procedures to follow during an interview. Our purpose is to point out some things you can do in advance that will help you and some good rules to follow and pitfalls to avoid while you are being interviewed.

What is an interview supposed to test?

The written examination is designed to test the technical knowledge and competence of the candidate; the oral is designed to evaluate intangible qualities, not readily measured otherwise, and to establish a list showing the relative fitness of each candidate – as measured against his competitors – for the position sought. Scoring is not on the basis of "right" and "wrong," but on a sliding scale of values ranging from "not passable" to "outstanding." As a matter of fact, it is possible to achieve a relatively low score without a single "incorrect" answer because of evident weakness in the qualities being measured.

Occasionally, an examination may consist entirely of an oral test – either an individual or a group oral. In such cases, information is sought concerning the technical knowledges and abilities of the candidate, since there has been no written examination for this purpose. More commonly, however, an oral test is used to supplement a written examination.

Who conducts interviews?

The composition of oral boards varies among different jurisdictions. In nearly all, a representative of the personnel department serves as chairman. One of the members of the board may be a representative of the department in which the candidate would work. In some cases, "outside experts" are used, and, frequently, a businessman or some other representative of the general public is asked to serve. Labor and management or other special groups may be represented. The aim is to secure the services of experts in the appropriate field.

However the board is composed, it is a good idea (and not at all improper or unethical) to ascertain in advance of the interview who the members are and what groups they represent. When you are introduced to them, you will have some idea of their backgrounds and interests, and at least you will not stutter and stammer over their names.

What should be done before the interview?

While knowledge about the board members is useful and takes some of the surprise element out of the interview, there is other preparation which is more substantive. It *is* possible to prepare for an oral interview – in several ways:

1) Keep a copy of your application and review it carefully before the interview

This may be the only document before the oral board, and the starting point of the interview. Know what education and experience you have listed there, and the sequence and dates of all of it. Sometimes the board will ask you to review the highlights of your experience for them; you should not have to hem and haw doing it.

2) Study the class specification and the examination announcement

Usually, the oral board has one or both of these to guide them. The qualities, characteristics or knowledges required by the position sought are stated in these documents. They offer valuable clues as to the nature of the oral interview. For example, if the job involves supervisory responsibilities, the announcement will usually indicate that knowledge of modern supervisory methods and the qualifications of the candidate as a supervisor will be tested. If so, you can expect such questions, frequently in the form of a hypothetical situation which you are expected to solve. NEVER go into an oral without knowledge of the duties and responsibilities of the job you seek.

3) Think through each qualification required

Try to visualize the kind of questions you would ask if you were a board member. How well could you answer them? Try especially to appraise your own knowledge and background in each area, *measured against the job sought*, and identify any areas in which you are weak. Be critical and realistic – do not flatter yourself.

4) Do some general reading in areas in which you feel you may be weak

For example, if the job involves supervision and your past experience has NOT, some general reading in supervisory methods and practices, particularly in the field of human relations, might be useful. Do NOT study agency procedures or detailed manuals. The oral board will be testing your understanding and capacity, not your memory.

5) Get a good night's sleep and watch your general health and mental attitude

You will want a clear head at the interview. Take care of a cold or any other minor ailment, and of course, no hangovers.

What should be done on the day of the interview?

Now comes the day of the interview itself. Give yourself plenty of time to get there. Plan to arrive somewhat ahead of the scheduled time, particularly if your appointment is in the fore part of the day. If a previous candidate fails to appear, the board might be ready for you a bit early. By early afternoon an oral board is almost invariably behind schedule if there are many candidates, and you may have to wait. Take along a book or magazine to read, or your application to review, but leave any extraneous material in the waiting room when you go in for your interview. In any event, relax and compose yourself.

The matter of dress is important. The board is forming impressions about you – from your experience, your manners, your attitude, and your appearance. Give your personal appearance careful attention. Dress your best, but not your flashiest. Choose conservative, appropriate clothing, and be sure it is immaculate. This is a business interview, and your appearance should indicate that you regard it as such. Besides, being well groomed and properly dressed will help boost your confidence.

Sooner or later, someone will call your name and escort you into the interview room. *This is it.* From here on you are on your own. It is too late for any more preparation. But remember, you asked for this opportunity to prove your fitness, and you are here because your request was granted.

What happens when you go in?

The usual sequence of events will be as follows: The clerk (who is often the board stenographer) will introduce you to the chairman of the oral board, who will introduce you to the other members of the board. Acknowledge the introductions before you sit down. Do not be surprised if you find a microphone facing you or a stenotypist sitting by. Oral interviews are usually recorded in the event of an appeal or other review.

Usually the chairman of the board will open the interview by reviewing the highlights of your education and work experience from your application – primarily for the benefit of the other members of the board, as well as to get the material into the record. Do not interrupt or comment unless there is an error or significant misinterpretation; if that is the case, do not hesitate. But do not quibble about insignificant matters. Also, he will usually ask you some question about your education, experience or your present job – partly to get you to start talking and to establish the interviewing "rapport." He may start the actual questioning, or turn it over to one of the other members. Frequently, each member undertakes the questioning on a particular area, one in which he is perhaps most competent, so you can expect each member to participate in the examination. Because time is limited, you may also expect some rather abrupt switches in the direction the questioning takes, so do not be upset by it. Normally, a board member will not pursue a single line of questioning unless he discovers a particular strength or weakness.

After each member has participated, the chairman will usually ask whether any member has any further questions, then will ask you if you have anything you wish to add. Unless you are expecting this question, it may floor you. Worse, it may start you off on an extended, extemporaneous speech. The board is not usually seeking more information. The question is principally to offer you a last opportunity to present further qualifications or to indicate that you have nothing to add. So, if you feel that a significant qualification or characteristic has been overlooked, it is proper to point it out in a sentence or so. Do not compliment the board on the thoroughness of their examination – they have been sketchy, and you know it. If you wish, merely say, "No thank you, I have nothing further to add." This is a point where you can "talk yourself out" of a good impression or fail to present an important bit of information. Remember, *you close the interview yourself.*

The chairman will then say, "That is all, Mr. _____, thank you." Do not be startled; the interview is over, and quicker than you think. Thank him, gather your belongings and take your leave. Save your sigh of relief for the other side of the door.

How to put your best foot forward

Throughout this entire process, you may feel that the board individually and collectively is trying to pierce your defenses, seek out your hidden weaknesses and embarrass and confuse you. Actually, this is not true. They are obliged to make an appraisal of your qualifications for the job you are seeking, and they want to see you in your best light. Remember, they must interview all candidates and a non-cooperative candidate may become a failure in spite of their best efforts to bring out his qualifications. Here are 15 suggestions that will help you:

1) Be natural – Keep your attitude confident, not cocky

If you are not confident that you can do the job, do not expect the board to be. Do not apologize for your weaknesses, try to bring out your strong points. The board is interested in a positive, not negative, presentation. Cockiness will antagonize any board member and make him wonder if you are covering up a weakness by a false show of strength.

2) Get comfortable, but don't lounge or sprawl

Sit erectly but not stiffly. A careless posture may lead the board to conclude that you are careless in other things, or at least that you are not impressed by the importance of the occasion. Either conclusion is natural, even if incorrect. Do not fuss with your clothing, a pencil or an ashtray. Your hands may occasionally be useful to emphasize a point; do not let them become a point of distraction.

3) Do not wisecrack or make small talk

This is a serious situation, and your attitude should show that you consider it as such. Further, the time of the board is limited – they do not want to waste it, and neither should you.

4) Do not exaggerate your experience or abilities

In the first place, from information in the application or other interviews and sources, the board may know more about you than you think. Secondly, you probably will not get away with it. An experienced board is rather adept at spotting such a situation, so do not take the chance.

5) If you know a board member, do not make a point of it, yet do not hide it

Certainly you are not fooling him, and probably not the other members of the board. Do not try to take advantage of your acquaintanceship – it will probably do you little good.

6) Do not dominate the interview

Let the board do that. They will give you the clues – do not assume that you have to do all the talking. Realize that the board has a number of questions to ask you, and do not try to take up all the interview time by showing off your extensive knowledge of the answer to the first one.

7) Be attentive

You only have 20 minutes or so, and you should keep your attention at its sharpest throughout. When a member is addressing a problem or question to you, give him your undivided attention. Address your reply principally to him, but do not exclude the other board members.

8) Do not interrupt

A board member may be stating a problem for you to analyze. He will ask you a question when the time comes. Let him state the problem, and wait for the question.

9) Make sure you understand the question

Do not try to answer until you are sure what the question is. If it is not clear, restate it in your own words or ask the board member to clarify it for you. However, do not haggle about minor elements.

10) Reply promptly but not hastily

A common entry on oral board rating sheets is "candidate responded readily," or "candidate hesitated in replies." Respond as promptly and quickly as you can, but do not jump to a hasty, ill-considered answer.

11) Do not be peremptory in your answers

A brief answer is proper – but do not fire your answer back. That is a losing game from your point of view. The board member can probably ask questions much faster than you can answer them.

12) Do not try to create the answer you think the board member wants

He is interested in what kind of mind you have and how it works – not in playing games. Furthermore, he can usually spot this practice and will actually grade you down on it.

13) Do not switch sides in your reply merely to agree with a board member

Frequently, a member will take a contrary position merely to draw you out and to see if you are willing and able to defend your point of view. Do not start a debate, yet do not surrender a good position. If a position is worth taking, it is worth defending.

14) Do not be afraid to admit an error in judgment if you are shown to be wrong

The board knows that you are forced to reply without any opportunity for careful consideration. Your answer may be demonstrably wrong. If so, admit it and get on with the interview.

15) Do not dwell at length on your present job

The opening question may relate to your present assignment. Answer the question but do not go into an extended discussion. You are being examined for a *new* job, not your present one. As a matter of fact, try to phrase ALL your answers in terms of the job for which you are being examined.

Basis of Rating

Probably you will forget most of these "do's" and "don'ts" when you walk into the oral interview room. Even remembering them all will not ensure you a passing grade. Perhaps you did not have the qualifications in the first place. But remembering them will help you to put your best foot forward, without treading on the toes of the board members.

Rumor and popular opinion to the contrary notwithstanding, an oral board wants you to make the best appearance possible. They know you are under pressure – but they also want to see how you respond to it as a guide to what your reaction would be under the pressures of the job you seek. They will be influenced by the degree of poise you display, the personal traits you show and the manner in which you respond.

ABOUT THIS BOOK

This book contains tests divided into Examination Sections. Go through each test, answering every question in the margin. We have also attached a sample answer sheet at the back of the book that can be removed and used. At the end of each test look at the answer key and check your answers. On the ones you got wrong, look at the right answer choice and learn. Do not fill in the answers first. Do not memorize the questions and answers, but understand the answer and principles involved. On your test, the questions will likely be different from the samples. Questions are changed and new ones added. If you understand these past questions you should have success with any changes that arise. Tests may consist of several types of questions. We have additional books on each subject should more study be advisable or necessary for you. Finally, the more you study, the better prepared you will be. This book is intended to be the last thing you study before you walk into the examination room. Prior study of relevant texts is also recommended. NLC publishes some of these in our Fundamental Series. Knowledge and good sense are important factors in passing your exam. Good luck also helps. So now study this Passbook, absorb the material contained within and take that knowledge into the examination. Then do your best to pass that exam.

EXAMINATION SECTION

EXAMINATION SECTION
TEST 1

DIRECTIONS: Each question or incomplete statement is followed by several suggested answers or completions. Select the one that BEST answers the question or completes the statement. *PRINT THE LETTER OF THE CORRECT ANSWER IN THE SPACE AT THE RIGHT.*

Questions 1-6.

DIRECTIONS: Questions 1 through 6 consist of descriptions of material to which a filing designation must be assigned.

Assume that the matters and cases described in the questions were referred for handling to a government legal office which has its files set up according to these file designations. The file designation consists of a number of characters and punctuation marks as described below.

The first character refers to agencies whose legal work is handled by this office. These agencies are numbered consecutively in the order in which they first submit a matter for attention, and are identified in an alphabetical card index. To date numbers have been assigned to agencies as follows:

Department of Correction	1
Police Department	2
Department of Traffic	3
Department of Consumer Affairs	4
Commission on Human Rights	5
Board of Elections	6
Department of Personnel	7
Board of Estimate	8

The second character is separated from the first character by a dash. The second character is the last digit of the year in which a particular lawsuit or matter is referred to the legal office.

The third character is separated from the second character by a colon and may consist of either of the following:

I. A sub-number assigned to each lawsuit to which the agency is a party. Lawsuits are numbered consecutively regardless of year. (Lawsuits are brought by or against agency heads rather than agencies themselves, but references are made to agencies for the purpose of simplification.)

or II. A capital letter assigned to each matter other than a lawsuit according to subject, the subject being identified in an alphabetical index. To date, letters have been assigned to subjects as follows:

Citizenship	A	Housing	E
Discrimination	B	Gambling	F
Residence Requirements	C	Freedom of Religion	G
Civil Service Examinations	D		

These referrals are numbered consecutively regardless of year. The first referral by a particular agency on citizenship, for example, would be designated A1, followed by A2, A3, etc.

If no reference is made in a question as to how many letters involving a certain subject or how many lawsuits have been referred by an agency, assume that it is the first.

For each question, choose the file designation which is MOST appropriate for filing the material described in the question.

1. In January 2010, two candidates in a 2009 civil service examination for positions with the Department of Correction filed a suit against the Department of Personnel seeking to set aside an educational requirement for the title.
   The Department of Personnel immediately referred the lawsuit to the legal office for handling.

   A. 1-9:1   B. 1-0:D1   C. 7-9:D1   D. 7-0:1

2. In 2014, the Police Department made its sixth request for an opinion on whether an employee assignment proposed for 2015 could be considered discriminatory.

   A. 2-5:1-B6   B. 2-4:6   C. 2-4:1-B6   D. 2-4:B6

3. In 2015, a lawsuit was brought by the Bay Island Action Committee against the Board of Estimate in which the plaintiff sought withdrawal of approval of housing for the elderly in the Bay Island area given by the Board in 2015.

   A. 8-3:1   B. 8-5:1   C. 8-3:B1   D. 8-5:E1

4. In December 2014, community leaders asked the Police Department to ban outdoor meetings of a religious group on the grounds that the meetings were disrupting the area. Such meetings had been held from time to time during 2014. On January 31, 2015, the Police Department asked the government legal office for an opinion on whether granting this request would violate the worshippers' right to freedom of religion.

   A. 2-4:G-1   B. 2-5:G1   C. 2-5:B-1   D. 2-4:B1

5. In 2014, a woman filed suit against the Board of Elections. She alleged that she had not been permitted to vote at her usual polling place in the 2013 election and had been told she was not registered there. She claimed that she had always voted there and that her record card had been lost. This was the fourth case of its type for this agency.

   A. 6-4:4   B. 6-3:C4   C. 3-4:6   D. 6-3:4

6. A lawsuit was brought in 2011 by the Ace Pinball Machine Company against the Commissioner of Consumer Affairs. The lawsuit contested an ordinance which banned the use of pinball machines on the ground that they are gambling devices.
   This was the third lawsuit to which the Department of Consumer Affairs was a party.

   A. 4-1:1   B. 4-3:F1   C. 4-1:3   D. 3F-4:1

7. You are instructed by your supervisor to type a statement that must be signed by the person making the statement and by three witnesses to the signature. The typed statement will take two pages and will leave no room for signatures if the normal margin is maintained at the bottom of the second page.
In this situation, the PREFERRED method is to type

   A. the signature lines below the normal margin on the second page
   B. nothing further and have the witnesses sign without a typed signature line
   C. the signature lines on a third page
   D. some of the text and the signature lines on a third page

8. Certain legal documents always begin with a statement of venue - that is, the county and state in which the document is executed. This is usually boxed with a parentheses or colons.
The one of the following documents that ALWAYS bears a statement of venue in a prominent position at its head is a(n)

   A. affidavit   B. memorandum of law
   C. contract of sale   D. will

9. A court stenographer is to take stenographic notes and transcribe the statements of a person under oath. The person has a heavy accent and speaks in ungrammatical and broken English.
When he or she is transcribing the testimony, of the following, the BEST thing for them to do is to

   A. transcribe the testimony exactly as spoken, making no grammatical changes
   B. make only the grammatical changes which would clarify the client's statements
   C. make all grammatical changes so that the testimony is in standard English form
   D. ask the client's permission before making any grammatical changes

10. When the material typed on a printed form does not fill the space provided, a Z-ruling is frequently drawn to fill up the unused space.
The MAIN purpose of this practice is to

    A. make the document more pleasing to the eye
    B. indicate that the preceding material is correct
    C. insure that the document is not altered
    D. show that the lawyer has read it

11. After you had typed an original and five copies of a certain document, some changes were made in ink on the original and were initialed by all the parties. The original was signed by all the parties, and the signatures were notarized.
Which of the following should *generally* be typed on the copies BEFORE filing the original and the copies? The inked changes

    A. but not the signatures, initials, or notarial data
    B. the signatures and the initials but not the notarial data
    C. and the notarial data but not the signatures or initials
    D. the signatures, the initials, and the notarial data

12. The first paragraph of a noncourt agreement *generally* contains all of the following EXCEPT the

    A. specific terms of the agreement
    B. date of the agreement
    C. purpose of the agreement
    D. names of the parties involved

13. When typing an answer in a court proceeding, the place where the word ANSWER should be typed on the first page of the document is

    A. at the upper left-hand corner
    B. below the index number and to the right of the box containing the names of the parties to the action
    C. above the index number and to the right of the box containing the names of the parties to the action
    D. to the left of the names of the attorneys for the defendant

14. Which one of the following statements BEST describes the legal document called an acknowledgment?
    It is

    A. an answer to an affidavit
    B. a receipt issued by the court when a document is filed
    C. proof of service of a summons
    D. a declaration that a signature is valid

15. Suppose you typed the original and three copies of a legal document which was dictated by an attorney in your office. He has already signed the original copy, and corrections have been made on all copies.
    Regarding the copies, which one of the following procedures is the PROPER one to follow?

    A. Leave the signature line blank on the copies
    B. Ask the attorney to sign the copies
    C. Print or type the attorney's name on the signature line on the copies
    D. Sign your name to the copies followed by the attorney's initials

16. Suppose your office is defending a particular person in a court action. This person comes to the office and asks to see some of the lawyer's working papers in his file. The lawyer assigned to the case is out of the office at the time.
    You SHOULD

    A. permit him to examine his entire file as long as he does not remove any materials from it
    B. make an appointment for the caller to come back later when the lawyer will be there
    C. ask him what working papers he wants to see and show him only those papers
    D. tell him that he needs written permission from the lawyer in order to see any records

17. Suppose that you receive a phone call from an official who is annoyed about a letter from your office which she just received. The lawyer who dictated the letter is not in the office at the moment.
Of the following, the BEST action for you to take is to

    A. explain that the lawyer is out but that you will ask the lawyer to return her call when he returns
    B. take down all of the details of her complaint and tell her that you will get back to her with an explanation
    C. refer to the proper file so that you can give her an explanation of the reasons for the letter over the phone
    D. make an appointment for her to stop by the office to speak with the lawyer

18. Suppose that you have taken dictation for an interoffice memorandum. You are asked to prepare it for distribution to four lawyers in your department whose names are given to you. You will type an original and make four copies. Which one of the following is CORRECT with regard to the typing of the lawyers' names?
The names of all of the lawyers should appear

    A. *only* on the original
    B. on the original and each copy should have the name of one lawyer
    C. on each of the copies but not on the original
    D. on the original and on all of the copies

19. Regarding the correct typing of punctuation, the GENERALLY accepted practice is that there should be

    A. two spaces after a semi-colon
    B. one space before an apostrophe used in the body of a word
    C. no space between parentheses and the matter enclosed
    D. one space before and after a hyphen

20. Suppose you have just completed typing an original and two copies of a letter requesting information. The original is to be signed by a lawyer in your office. The first copy is for the files, and the second is to be used as a reminder to follow up.
The PROPER time to file the file copy of the letter is

    A. after the letter has been signed and corrections have been made on the copies
    B. before you take the letter to the lawyer for his signature
    C. after a follow-up letter has been sent
    D. after a response to the letter has been received

21. A secretary in a legal office has just typed a letter. She has typed the copy distribution notation on the copies to indicate *blind copy distribution*. This *blind copy* notation shows that

    A. copies of the letter are being sent to persons that the addressee does not know
    B. copies of the letter are being sent to other persons without the addressee's knowledge
    C. a copy of the letter will be enlarged for a legally blind person
    D. a copy of the letter is being given as an extra copy to the addressee

22. Suppose that one of the attorneys in your office dictates material to you without indicating punctuation. He has asked that you give him, as soon as possible, a single copy of a rough draft to be triple-spaced so that he can make corrections.
Of the following, what is the BEST thing for you to do in this situation?

   A. Assume that no punctuation is desired in the material
   B. Insert the punctuation as you type the rough draft
   C. Transcribe the material exactly as dictated, but attach a note to the attorney stating your suggested changes
   D. Before you start to type the draft, tell the attorney you want to read back your notes so that he can indicate punctuation

23. When it is necessary to type a mailing notation such as CERTIFIED, REGISTERED, or FEDEX on an envelope, the GENERALLY accepted place to type it is

   A. directly above the address
   B. in the area below where the stamp will be affixed
   C. in the lower left-hand corner
   D. in the upper left-hand corner

24. When taking a citation of a case in shorthand, which of the following should you write FIRST if you are having difficulty keeping up with the dictation?

   A. Volume and page number   B. Title of volume
   C. Name of plaintiff   D. Name of defendant

25. All of the following abbreviations and their meanings are correctly paired EXCEPT

   A. viz. - namely   B. ibid. - refer
   C. n.b. - note well   D. q.v. - which see

KEY (CORRECT ANSWERS)

1. D		11. D	
2. D		12. A	
3. B		13. B	
4. B		14. D	
5. A		15. C	
6. C		16. B	
7. D		17. A	
8. A		18. D	
9. A		19. C	
10. C		20. A	

21. B
22. B
23. B
24. A
25. B

EXAMINATION SECTION
TEST 1

DIRECTIONS: Each question or incomplete statement is followed by several suggested answers or completions. Select the one that BEST answers the question or completes the statement. *PRINT THE LETTER OF THE CORRECT ANSWER IN THE SPACE AT THE RIGHT.*

Questions 1-9.

DIRECTIONS: Questions 1 through 9 consist of sentences which may or may not be examples of good English usage. Consider grammar, punctuation, spelling, capitalization, awkwardness, etc. Examine each sentence, and then choose the correct statement about it from the four choices below it. If the English usage in the sentence given is better than it would be with any of the changes suggested in options B, C, and D, choose option A. Do not choose an option that will change the meaning of the sentence.

1. According to Judge Frank, the grocer's sons found guilty of assault and sentenced last Thursday.   1.____

    A. This is an example of acceptable writing.
    B. A comma should be placed after the word *sentenced.*
    C. The word *were* should be placed after *sons*
    D. The apostrophe in *grocer's* should be placed after the *s.*

2. The department heads assistant said that the stenographers should type duplicate copies of all contracts, leases, and bills.   2.____

    A. This is an example of acceptable writing.
    B. A comma should be placed before the word *contracts.*
    C. An apostrophe should be placed before the *s* in *heads.*
    D. Quotation marks should be placed before *the stenographers* and after *bills.*

3. The lawyers questioned the men to determine who was the true property owner?   3.____

    A. This is an example of acceptable writing.
    B. The phrase *questioned the men* should be changed to *asked the men questions.*
    C. The word *was* should be changed to *were.*
    D. The question mark should be changed to a period.

4. The terms stated in the present contract are more specific than those stated in the previous contract.   4.____

    A. This is an example of acceptable writing.
    B. The word *are* should be changed to *is.*
    C. The word *than* should be changed to *then.*
    D. The word *specific* should be changed to *specified.*

5. Of the lawyers considered, the one who argued more skillful was chosen for the job.   5.____

    A. This is an example of acceptable writing.
    B. The word *more* should be replaced by the word *most.*
    C. The word *skillful* should be replaced by the word *skillfully,*
    D. The word *chosen* should be replaced by the word *selected.*

6. Each of the states has a court of appeals; some states have circuit courts. 6.____

   A. This is an example of acceptable writing.
   B. The semi-colon should be changed to a comma.
   C. The word *has* should be changed to *have*.
   D. The word *some* should be capitalized.

7. The court trial has greatly effected the child's mental condition. 7.____

   A. This is an example of acceptable writing.
   B. The word *effected* should be changed to *affected*.
   C. The word *greatly* should be placed after *effected*.
   D. The apostrophe in *child's* should be placed after the *s*.

8. Last week, the petition signed by all the officers was sent to the Better Business Bureau. 8.____

   A. This is an example of acceptable writing.
   B. The phrase *last week* should be placed after *officers*.
   C. A comma should be placed after *petition*.
   D. The word *was* should be changed to *were*.

9. Mr. Farrell claims that he requested form A-12, and three booklets describing court procedures. 9.____

   A. This is an example of acceptable writing.
   B. The word *that* should be eliminated.
   C. A colon should be placed after *requested*.
   D. The comma after *A-12* should be eliminated.

Questions 10-21.

DIRECTIONS: Questions 10 through 21 contain a word in capital letters followed by four suggested meanings of the word. For each question, choose the BEST meaning for the word in capital letters.

10. SIGNATORY - A 10.____

    A. lawyer who draws up a legal document
    B. document that must be signed by a judge
    C. person who signs a document
    D. true copy of a signature

11. RETAINER - A 11.____

    A. fee paid to a lawyer for his services
    B. document held by a third party
    C. court decision to send a prisoner back to custody pending trial
    D. legal requirement to keep certain types of files

12. BEQUEATH - To 12.____

    A. receive assistance from a charitable organization
    B. give personal property by will to another
    C. transfer real property from one person to another
    D. receive an inheritance upon the death of a relative

13. RATIFY - To   13.____
    A. approve and sanction   B. forego
    C. produce evidence   D. summarize

14. CODICIL - A   14.____
    A. document introduced in evidence in a civil action
    B. subsection of a law
    C. type of legal action that can be brought by a plaintiff
    D. supplement or an addition to a will

15. ALIAS   15.____
    A. Assumed name   B. In favor of
    C. Against   D. A writ

16. PROXY - A(n)   16.____
    A. phony document in a real estate transaction
    B. opinion by a judge of a civil court
    C. document containing appointment of an agent
    D. summons in a lawsuit

17. ALLEGED   17.____
    A. Innocent   B. Asserted
    C. Guilty   D. Called upon

18. EXECUTE - To   18.____
    A. complete a legal document by signing it
    B. set requirements
    C. render services to a duly elected executive of a municipality
    D. initiate legal action such as a lawsuit

19. NOTARY PUBLIC - A   19.____
    A. lawyer who is running for public office
    B. judge who hears minor cases
    C. public officer, one of whose functions is to administer oaths
    D. lawyer who gives free legal services to persons unable to pay

20. WAIVE - To   20.____
    A. disturb a calm state of affairs
    B. knowingly renounce a right or claim
    C. pardon someone for a minor fault
    D. purposely mislead a person during an investigation

21. ARRAIGN - To   21.____
    A. prevent an escape   B. defend a prisoner
    C. verify a document   D. accuse in a court of law

Questions 22-40.

DIRECTIONS: Questions 22 through 40 each consist of four words which may or may not be spelled correctly. If you find an error in
only one word, mark your answer A;
any two words, mark your answer B;
any three words, mark your answer C;
none of these words, mark your answer D.

22.	occurrence	Febuary	privilege	similiar	22._____
23.	separate	transferring	analyze	column	23._____
24.	develop	license	bankrupcy	abreviate	24._____
25.	subpoena	arguement	dissolution	foreclosure	25._____
26.	exaggerate	fundamental	significance	warrant	26._____
27.	citizen	endorsed	marraige	appraissal	27._____
28.	precedant	univercity	observence	preliminary	28._____
29.	stipulate	negligence	judgment	prominent	29._____
30.	judisial	whereas	release	guardian	30._____
31.	appeal	larcenny	transcrip	jurist	31._____
32.	petition	tenancy	agenda	insurance	32._____
33.	superfical	premise	morgaged	maintainance	33._____
34.	testamony	publically	installment	possessed	34._____
35.	escrow	decree	eviction	miscelaneous	35._____
36.	securitys	abeyance	adhere	corporate	36._____
37.	kaleidoscope	anesthesia	vermilion	tafetta	37._____
38.	congruant	barrenness	plebescite	vigilance	38._____
39.	picnicing	promisory	resevoir	omission	39._____
40.	supersede	banister	wholly	seize	40._____

KEY (CORRECT ANSWERS)

1. C	11. A	21. D	31. B
2. C	12. B	22. B	32. D
3. D	13. A	23. D	33. C
4. A	14. D	24. B	34. B
5. C	15. A	25. A	35. A
6. A	16. C	26. D	36. A
7. B	17. B	27. B	37. A
8. A	18. A	28. C	38. B
9. D	19. C	29. D	39. C
10. C	20. B	30. A	40. D

EXAMINATION SECTION
TEST 1

DIRECTIONS: Each question or incomplete statement is followed by several suggested answers or completions. Select the one that BEST answers the question or completes the statement. *PRINT THE LETTER OF THE CORRECT ANSWER IN THE SPACE AT THE RIGHT.*

1. An affidavit and a summons are similar in that an affidavit and a summons
    A. both require an answer
    B. both may be filed with a court of proper jurisdiction
    C. outline the particulars of the case
    D. are both served on each party in a lawsuit

2. A judgment of the court refers to a(n)
    A. final order and decision on a matter before the Court that is binding on both parties
    B. reservation by the judge to defer a decision to a later date
    C. award by the judge granting monetary payment to the plaintiff
    D. request by the defendant to dismiss the case against the plaintiff

3. A pretrial conference typically requires the presence of the
    A. attorneys representing the parties and the case and the judge
    B. judge only
    C. named parties in the lawsuit and the judge
    D. named parties in the lawsuit, attorneys, and the judge

4. Gary, a local business owner, has discovered one of his customers is suing him for monetary and punitive damages in court. Gary would like to represent himself at trial.
    Gary is a(n) _____ litigant.
    A. Qui Tam   B. In Limine   C. Pro Se   D. Pro Tem

5. A subpoena duces tecum requires its recipient to
    A. appear and produce documents   B. appear and provide testimony
    C. appear with a witness   D. appear

6. A capital offense is characterized by its punishment. A capital offense is punishable by
    A. large money payment, payable in a lump sum
    B. lien on real property
    C. death
    D. an automatic sentence of 20 years

7. Bankruptcy law is governed by _____ law, rather than _____ law. Therefore, bankruptcy hearings are heard in _____ courts.
   A. State, Federal, District
   B. District, State, Federal
   C. Federal, District, State
   D. Federal, State, District

7._____

8. Michelle is the subject of a wage garnishment. She is a full-time student at Brooklyn College and also works full time as an administrative assistant for an accountant in Queens. After receiving notice of the wage garnishment, she decides to quit her job and take a part-time job as a receptionist at a dental office.
   Are Michelle's dental office wages subject to garnishment?
   A. No, because she is only working part time.
   B. No, because the garnishment was issued while she was working at her last job.
   C. Yes, because she obtained new employment.
   D. Yes.

8._____

9. A trial which was scheduled to begin in Queens in October is now being moved to Albany. The trial is still scheduled to begin in October.
   The change of the trial location is an example of a change in
   A. venue
   B. locale
   C. environment
   D. jurisdiction

9._____

10. Plaintiff's attorney has withdrawn as counsel and is being replaced by another attorney who comes highly recommended by a family friend of the plaintiff.
    Where is the change of attorney MOST appropriately recorded?
    A. Disclosure statement
    B. Docket
    C. Letter to the Judge
    D. Deposition

10._____

11. A bench trial is a trial without a(n)
    A. plaintiff's attorney
    B. jury
    C. defendant's attorney
    D. bailiff

11._____

12. Mark's son, Jeff, has been arrested and is being held on $50,000 bail. Mark is visibly upset and angrily demands to know why bail is required in order for Jeff to be released from prison.
    The MOST correct answer is:
    A. Bail is absolutely required of all prisoners awaiting trial.
    B. Bail is required to release Jeff because he committed a felony.
    C. Bail is not always required, but can be established to ensure a person's appearance at court when required.
    D. Bail is only required when a probation officer has not yet been assigned.

12._____

13. In classifying her debts in bankruptcy, Alicia attests that she owes $10,000 in personal credit card debt, $5,000 business loan to a credit union, and $200,000 mortgage.
    Which debts will be classified as consumer debt?
    A. Credit card debt, business loan, and mortgage
    B. The business loan only
    C. Credit card debt and business loans
    D. Credit card debt and mortgage

13.____

14. A warrant has been issued by Judge Walker for John Smith. There are typically two types of warrants that can be issued.
    They are
    A. search and arrest
    B. seize and arrest
    C. detain and arrest
    D. summons and arrest

14.____

15. The role of the court stenographer is to
    A. assist the bailiff in maintaining order in the courtroom
    B. serve as an additional support to the court clerk
    C. transcribe the dialogue of court proceedings in short form to create the trial transcript
    D. record the final judgment and transcribe the judge's rationale for sentencing

15.____

16. Precedent refers to:
    A. The same plaintiff and same defendant from another lawsuit are named in the present suit
    B. A defendant is on trial again after being found innocent in an earlier trial
    C. An earlier case or decision of a court that is considered authority in the present case because of an identical or similar question of law
    D. A series of lawsuits involving the same plaintiff in each case

16.____

17. An automatic stay has what effect on a debtor in a bankruptcy petition?
    A. Allows the debtor to appoint a trustee for his/her petition
    B. Stops lawsuits, foreclosures, garnishments, and most collection activities against the debtor the moment a bankruptcy petition is filed
    C. Provides the debtor with additional time to arrange their assets before filing the petition
    D. Allows the debtor to attend court hearings on the status of their bankruptcy petition

17.____

18. A joint petition in bankruptcy refers to a bankruptcy
    A. petition filed by a husband and wife together
    B. petition filed by business partners
    C. petition filed by family members
    D. petitioned by the largest creditor of the debtor

18.____

19. A misdemeanor is punishable by _____ or _____, whereas a felony is punishable by _____ or _____.
    A. two years, less; two years, more
    B. six months, less; six months, more
    C. one year, less; one year, more
    D. one year, more; one year, less

20. Gail has filed for Chapter 7 bankruptcy. She has read online that some of her property will be considered non-exempt assets.
    Non-exempt assets is property that
    A. can be sold to satisfy claims of the creditors
    B. is exempt from being included in the bankruptcy estate
    C. does not need to be reported to the trustee
    D. can be considered "charge offs" for tax purposes

21. A motion represents a _____ to the court, requiring a decision by the judge.
    A. request   B. demand   C. action   D. plea

22. A jury verdict that a criminal defendant is not guilty, or a finding by a judge that there is insufficient evidence to support a conviction is known as a(n)
    A. information
    B. acquiescence
    C. acquittal
    D. compromise in settlement

23. An affidavit is accurately defined as a(n)
    A. statement made in the presence of a court of competent jurisdiction
    B. written statement that is notarized then sent to a court of competent jurisdiction
    C. oral statement transcribed by his or her attorney
    D. written or printed statement made under oath

24. Under what circumstances does an alternate juror help decide a case?
    A. Only when called on to replace a regular juror
    B. When a regular juror has trouble making a decision in the case
    C. When the bailiff asks the alternate jurors' opinion on the case
    D. Only during bench trials

25. A case that is dismissed with prejudice prevents which of the following:
    The filing of
    A. an identical suit in a later filing
    B. a suit by the same plaintiff in a later filing
    C. a suit by the same defendant in a later filing
    D. the same suit in the same courthouse in a later filing

KEY (CORRECT ANSWERS)

1.	B	11.	B
2.	A	12.	C
3.	A	13.	D
4.	C	14.	A
5.	A	15.	C
6.	C	16.	C
7.	D	17.	B
8.	D	18.	A
9.	A	19.	C
10.	B	20.	A

21.	A
22.	C
23.	D
24.	A
25.	A

TEST 2

DIRECTIONS: Each question or incomplete statement is followed by several suggested answers or completions. Select the one that BEST answers the question or completes the statement. *PRINT THE LETTER OF THE CORRECT ANSWER IN THE SPACE AT THE RIGHT.*

1. There are various forms of discovery that can be requested by either party in a lawsuit.
   _____ is the form of discovery that consists of written questions that are answered in writing and under oath.
   A. Depositions
   B. Examinations before trial
   C. Interrogatories
   D. Affidavits

   1._____

2. At what point in a trial are jury instructions delivered by the judge?
   A. Before the trial begins
   B. After opening arguments
   C. After the defense rests
   D. Before the jury is to begin deliberations

   2._____

3. In a bench trial, the _____ serves as the fact finder.
   A. jury   B. judge   C. bailiff   D. law clerk

   3._____

4. The role of the bankruptcy trustee is to represent the
   A. interests of the bankruptcy estate and the creditors of the debtor
   B. debtor against all creditors
   C. largest creditor of the debtor
   D. small creditor of the debtor

   4._____

5. The bankruptcy estate typically includes _____ at the time of filing.
   A. all property of the debtor, including interests in real property
   B. the home where the debtor resides
   C. the home and personal vehicle of the debtor
   D. all personal property, but not real property, of the debtor

   5._____

6. An amicus curiae brief is filed by a person or entity with a(n) _____ in, but that is not a _____ in the case.
   A. outcome; party
   B. interest; party
   C. party; outcome
   D. party; interest

   6._____

7. An answer is a formal response to which document?
   A. Deposition   B. Discovery   C. Complaint   D. Advice

   7._____

8. Donovan sued his former employer, Ink Securities, LLC and his former boss, Steve, for unpaid wages. Ink Securities lost the case and now wishes to appeal the ruling.
   When Steve and Ink Securities, LLC appeal the case, what do they become?
   A. Appellees   B. Appellants   C. Plaintiffs   D. Defendants

   8._____

9. In an indictment or information, each count represents a(n)
   A. proven crime
   B. request by the court
   C. decision on the merits
   D. allegation

10. Allison is sentenced to six years for armed robbery and ten years for grand larceny. She is sentenced to serve her prison terms concurrently. What is the MAXIMUM amount of time Allison will spend behind bars?
    A. Six years
    B. Sixteen years
    C. Ten years
    D. Four years

11. An appellate review de novo is one that provides no _____ to the ruling of the trial judge.
    A. deference
    B. credibility
    C. assignability
    D. advancement

12. Mary Ellen's house is worth $700,000, her car is worth $10,000, and she has cash and other financial assets worth $50,000. Creditors in Mary Ellen's bankruptcy have secured an interest in Mary Ellen's personal and real property amounting to $650,000.
    How much equity remains in Mary Ellen's property?
    A. $90,000   B. $50,000   C. $10,000   D. $110,000

13. Ex parte communications are generally strictly forbidden because the
    A. other party is not privy to the information that is shared, creating the appearance of bias in a case
    B. associated cost to appeal a case with ex parte communications is an undue burden to the plaintiff
    C. defendant usually prevails when ex parte communications occur
    D. jury is not privy to the information that is shared, creating the appearance of bias in a case

14. What does the exclusionary rule exclude in a criminal trial?
    A. Testimony that is deemed hearsay by a judge in a court of competent jurisdiction
    B. Evidence obtained in violation of a defendant's constitutional or statutory rights
    C. Depositions that are unsworn or not notarized
    D. Affidavits that are unsworn or not notarized

15. Grand juries convene to determine whether there is _____ to believe an individual committed an offense.
    A. burden of proof
    B. reasonable belief
    C. probable cause
    D. an absolute determination

16. A liquidated claim is a claim that can be satisfied by
    A. a fixed amount of money
    B. real property
    C. personal property
    D. a percentage of property that will be sold

17. A motion to lift the automatic stay is a request to take action in a bankruptcy case that would otherwise violate the automatic stay.
    This motion is filed by the
    A. debtor's attorney
    B. bankruptcy trustee
    C. creditor(s)
    D. trustee's attorney

18. David is being arraigned and needs to enter a plea for the crime he allegedly committed while he was with his friend, Robert. Robert pleaded guilty during his arraignment yesterday, but David has been advised by his attorney to plead no contest, also known as
    A. nolo contendere
    B. pro se
    C. quid pro quo
    D. qui tam

19. Under federal law, a petty offense is any misdemeanor which is punishable by a period of _____ or less, a fine of not more than $5,000, or both.
    A. one year   B. six months   C. two years   D. 1 month

20. If a case is remanded by a Court of Appeals, what effect does this have on the case at bar?
    A. The attorneys on the case are replaced for both the plaintiff and defendant.
    B. The appellant becomes the appellee in a new trial.
    C. The case is sent back to the trial, or lower, court.
    D. The trial court has the right to enter a determination to the Court of Appeals which may materially affect the outcome of the case.

21. Sentencing Guidelines are set by which entity or government entity?
    A. The Bureau of Prisons
    B. Immigration and Customs Enforcement
    C. Department of Justice
    D. U.S. Sentencing Commission

22. Sequestered juries are prevented from
    A. being biased by outside influences during deliberations
    B. speaking with one another during deliberations
    C. relying on alternate juror votes in rendering a decision in a trial
    D. hearing testimony from witnesses deemed to have hearsay evidence

23. A statute is a law passed by the
    A. courts
    B. judicial branch
    C. legislature
    D. executive branch

24. If an element or issue in a case has not arisen, or no longer applies to the matter at hand because it has ended before trial, the issue is considered
    A. triable
    B. factual
    C. indeterminate
    D. moot

25. Susan would like to file a restraining order on her ex-husband, John, and may want to sue him criminally and civilly. She asks for advice on the rules of conducting a lawsuit.
These rules are otherwise known as
A. procedure B. terms C. requirements D. issues

25.____

KEY (CORRECT ANSWERS)

1. C
2. D
3. B
4. A
5. A

6. B
7. C
8. B
9. D
10. C

11. A
12. D
13. A
14. B
15. C

16. A
17. C
18. A
19. B
20. C

21. D
22. A
23. C
24. D
25. A

TEST 3

DIRECTIONS: Each question or incomplete statement is followed by several suggested answers or completions. Select the one that BEST answers the question or completes the statement. *PRINT THE LETTER OF THE CORRECT ANSWER IN THE SPACE AT THE RIGHT.*

1. The delivery of writs or summons to one party in a lawsuit is also known as
   A. demand for interrogatories
   B. requests for information
   C. service of process
   D. statement on the record

2. The time in which a lawsuit must be filed or a criminal prosecution must begin is called
   A. tolling period
   B. statute of limitations
   C. timely prosecution
   D. Article III hearing

3. A subpoena requires its recipient to appear and provide _____, while a subpoena duces tecum requires its recipient to appear and provide _____.
   A. documents; testimony
   B. a witness; testimony
   C. documents; a witness
   D. testimony; documents

4. _____ is the process of selecting a jury by questioning prospective jurors to ascertain their qualifications and determine if there is a basis for challenge, such as a conflict or other reason for disqualification.
   A. sua sponte
   B. de jure
   C. voir dire
   D. jury statement

5. In executing a warrant, law enforcement has court authorization to make an arrest, _____, or both.
   A. conduct a search
   B. question a suspect
   C. subpoena a suspect's attorney
   D. require a personal appearance by the suspect

6. A Chapter 7 case where there are no available assets of the debtor that would satisfy any portion of a creditor's unsecured claims is referred to as a(n)
   A. liquidation case
   B. no asset case
   C. unranked estate
   D. dischargeable debt

7. Bill and Tim are neighbors. They are currently engaged in a heated dispute over the boundary of the property line that separates their lots. Bill has sued Tim for harassment as he claims Tim parks his delivery truck in the driveway that is on Bill's property. A judge has issued a court order which prevents Tim from parking any vehicle in the driveway in dispute until further research can be completed by the attorneys for either side.
   The court order issued is
   A. injunction
   B. restraining order
   C. issue
   D. home confinement

8. If a case is dismissed without prejudice, that court has made no decision on the merits and the parties are allowed to
   A. question the final ruling
   B. file the case at a later date
   C. find new attorneys/representation
   D. ignore the final ruling

   8.____

9. May a deposition be used later in trial?
   A. Yes, but only if the witness was represented by an attorney
   B. Yes, as it is an oral statement made before an officer authorized by law to administer oaths
   C. No, because it is a written statement that can be retracted at any time
   D. No

   9.____

10. Madeline asks for advice regarding the discovery process. She is unsure what it entails.
    Discovery is the
    A. procedure that governs the exchange of information, particularly the disclosure of evidence, between the parties before trial
    B. procedure that governs the appearance of the testifying witnesses at trial
    C. rules of evidence both parties must adhere to during the trial
    D. exchange of motions and subpoenas before trial

    10.____

11. The docket is an important component of court proceedings because
    A. it is a log containing the complete history of each case
    B. it is accessible to the jury who can better understand the procedural history of each case.
    C. the judge enters the journal entries guaranteeing the docket's accuracy
    D. each court docket is at least 100 separate entries

    11.____

12. Information presented in testimony or in documents used to persuade a judge or jury in deciding a case in favor of one side or the other is termed
    A. disclosure   B. deposition   C. evidence   D. indictment

    12.____

13. Samuel is on trial for armed robbery. Samuel's attorney, Maxine, presents evidence her client was not in the state during the robbery and does not own a weapon of any kind.
    What kind of evidence is Maxine presenting to the court?
    A. Alibi
    B. Exculpatory
    C. Exclusionary
    D. Exemplary

    13.____

14. Samantha and Steven are separately called as witnesses in the trial of Adam Jones, who is being tried for murder. Steven testifies that he saw Adam commit the crime behind a local bar. Samantha testifies that Steven told her what Adam did.
    Adam's attorney objects to Samantha's testimony because it is
    A. exculpatory
    B. hearsay
    C. untrue
    D. impeachment

    14.____

15. After filing bankruptcy, Katherine sells her home to her daughter. Katherine's home is currently worth $300,000. She sells it to her daughter for $5. Katherine's sale of her home is deemed a
    A. insider transaction
    B. joint administration
    C. transfer of jurisprudence
    D. fraudulent transfer

    15.____

16. When a trial is deemed invalid and must start again with a new jury, the trial is called a
    A. acquittal
    B. mistrial
    C. in limine
    D. no asset case

    16.____

17. Oral arguments are an opportunity for _____ to summarize their position before the court.
    A. jurors
    B. plaintiffs
    C. the accused
    D. attorneys

    17.____

18. During jury selection, the judge grants each side the right to exclude a certain number of prospective jurors without reason. This grant is also called a _____ challenge.
    A. prospective
    B. per curiam
    C. peremptory
    D. petition

    18.____

19. Who prepares the pre-sentence report for the court?
    A. The plaintiff's attorney
    B. The jury
    c. The defendant's attorney
    D. The court's probation officer

    19.____

20. The legal doctrine that allows for the delay or pausing of the statute of limitations is referred to as
    A. extended delay
    B. tolling
    C. transferring
    D. tort

    20.____

21. At trial, William was convicted of harassment and the negligent infliction of emotional distress. His attorney appealed the decision to the Court of Appeals. The Court of Appeals disagreed with the lower court and acquitted William of all charges.
    The Court of Appeals _____ the lower court's decision.
    A. remanded
    b. reversed
    C. returned
    D. rescinded

    21.____

22. The preparation of schedules requires the disclosure of
    A. assets, liabilities, and other financial information
    B. past convicted crimes
    C. past arrests
    D. past employment

    22.____

23. The punishment ordered by a court for a defendant convicted of a crime is logged in the docket as the official
    A. disposition of the case
    B. sentence
    C. dismissal of the case
    D. order

    23.____

24. John's trial is set to begin a month before Judge Smith. In a pre-trial hearing, it is determined that John is not a resident of the state where the trial will take place, and the alleged crime was not committed in the state. Judge Smith quickly realizes the court does not have jurisdiction and dismisses the case so that it can be filed with a court of proper jurisdiction.
Judge Smith's action, without prompting from either the plaintiff or defendant, is referred to as
    A. per diem   B. pro tem   C. sua sponte   D. en banc

25. In criminal cases, prosecutors must prove a defendant's guilt beyond a reasonable doubt.
In most civil trials, the _____ is by a preponderance of the evidence.
    A. clear and convincing   B. standard of proof
    C. evidence   D. degree and necessity

KEY (CORRECT ANSWERS)

1. C		11. A	
2. B		12. C	
3. D		13. B	
4. C		14. B	
5. A		15. D	
6. B		16. B	
7. A		17. D	
8. B		18. C	
9. B		19. D	
10. A		20. B	

21. B
22. A
23. B
24. C
25. B

TEST 4

DIRECTIONS: Each question or incomplete statement is followed by several suggested answers or completions. Select the one that BEST answers the question or completes the statement. *PRINT THE LETTER OF THE CORRECT ANSWER IN THE SPACE AT THE RIGHT.*

1. The _____ is the final decision by the fact finder (judge or jury) that determines the guilt or innocence of a criminal defendant, or the outcome of a civil case.
    A. order
    B. punishment
    C. verdict
    D. decision

2. Following precedent, or adhering to the decisions in prior cases involving the same issue is known as _____, the Latin term meaning "to stand by things decided."
    A. pro tempura
    B. en banc
    C. stare decisis
    D. quid pro quo

3. One of the largest areas of civil law, a _____ is a wrongful or illegal act which causes injury to another.
    A. criminal
    B. tort
    C. defendant
    D. punitive

4. Stacy wants to sue Bob, who sold her a used car last year. Stacy alleges that Bob knowingly sold her a stolen car. Stacy paid Bob $5,000 for the car and in exchange Bob provided her with the keys to the car and a coupon for four free oil changes. No other documents were exchanged between Bob and Stacy.
   What document would prove who the legal owner of the car truly is?
    A. A wobbler
    B. Disclosure statement
    C. Schedule of ownership
    D. Title

5. Michelle walks into a local courthouse and demands to speak with the clerk. She is upset that her neighbor, Rich, has not picked up the leaves on his property all season. She feels strongly his failure to do so will drive property prices down and, additionally, the leaves keep blowing into her yard.
   The clerk informs Michelle that she is free to contact an attorney, but should know that she will not likely be able to proceed with a lawsuit because
    A. there is no cause of action
    B. the courts cannot force Rich to pick up his leaves or prevent the leaves from blowing onto Michelle's property
    C. the statute of limitations will pass by the time Michelle contacts an attorney
    D. punitive damages are not likely to be awarded, so filing a lawsuit will be frivolous

6. Latin for a "guilty mind," this term is synonymous with "intent" and for some crimes, it must be present when the person committed the criminal act in order to be found guilty.
   A. Pro se B. Mens rea C. Pro tem D. En banc

   6.____

7. Compensatory damages are different from punitive damages in that: Compensatory damages
   A. are recovered for injury or economic loss, while punitive are awarded over and above compensatory damages for the purpose of punishment and to serve as a deterrent to others
   B. and punitive damages both make the injured party whole, but compensatory damages can be up to 10% more than the actual claim
   C. serve as a deterrent to others, while punitive damages are recovered for injury or economic loss
   D. are incurred from the moment the crime occurs, thereby accruing interest, whereas punitive damages are awarded in a lump sum

   7.____

8. Malfeasance is defined as doing something illegal or morally wrong, and is usually associated with a(n)
   A. abuse of authority committed by a public official
   B. torts committed in a public setting
   C. crimes that are punishable by one year or more in prison
   D. a crime committed by a judge, court officer, or registered attorney

   8.____

9. A title abstract search on a home would provide the researcher with a
   A. list of people who made bids to buy the property
   B. list of real estate agents who worked on selling the home as well as a list of real estate agents representing potential buyers of the home
   C. history of ownership that establishes the present state of a title
   D. history of individuals who lived in the home at one point in time

   9.____

10. A crime that can be classified as either a felony or a misdemeanor is often referred to as a
    A. deciding factor   B. wobbler
    C. precedent   D. information

    10.____

11. A formal response to a complaint that pleads for dismissal due to a lack of a legal basis for a lawsuit is called
    A. an answer   B. an affidavit
    C. a motion in limine D. demurrer

    11.____

12. Administrative law concerns _____ agencies, such as the U.S. Department of Housing and Urban Development (HUD) or the U.S. Department of Education.
    A. government   B. municipal
    C. administrative   D. elected

    12.____

13. Daniel committed and is currently being sentenced for his involvement in an armed robbery. His attorney is seeking alternative sanctions given that Daniel was present during the commission of the crime, but did not actively participate.
    His attorney asks the court for
    A. alternative sanctions
    B. sentencing by statute
    C. diminished capacity
    D. demurrer

13.____

14. The attorney who appears in the permanent records or files of a case is known as the _____ unless he or she withdraws or is otherwise removed from the case.
    A. attorney of the case
    B. attorney of record
    C. attorney in time
    D. permanent attorney

14.____

15. Mark and Cindy are divorcing. Cindy did not request money for support from Mark prior to the final court hearing, therefore her rights to _____ are waived.
    A. child support
    B. compensatory damages
    C. punitive damages
    D. alimony

15.____

16. Attorneys for the plaintiff and the defendant agree that each side needs more time to conduct additional discovery before trial.
    The parties jointly request a(n)
    A. recess
    B. voir dire
    C. adjournment
    D. information

16.____

17. Instead of using a judge, amicable parties may decide to submit to _____ for a decision.
    A. adjudication
    B. arbitration
    C. meritorious decision
    D. jury trial

17.____

18. The first court appearance of a person accused of a crime, where he or she is advised of his or her rights is called a(n)
    A. plea meeting
    B. pretrial conference
    C. jury selection
    D. arraignment

18.____

19. Charlie is behind on his child support and alimony payments to his ex-wife, Miranda. The court garnishes his wages to satisfy the amount in _____ that is overdue and unpaid.
    A. arrears
    B. damages
    C. satisfaction
    D. lien

19.____

20. Joel became aware that he was being sued by his former business partner when he was served with a verified complaint by a process server last May. Joel decided to ignore the complaint altogether and believed that, eventually, the lawsuit would go away.
    What is Joel's status in the suit?
    A. He owes his former business partner punitive damages, because he failed to respond or answer.
    B. He is a defendant that will be forced to go to trial to answer to the charges.
    C. He is in default as he failed to answer or respond to the plaintiff's claims.
    D. He is in limbo as he did not answer the complaint but the trial date has not yet been set.

21. The permanent home of a person is referred to as their _____; where a person can have many residences, they can only have one of these.
    A. domicile
    B. address
    C. place of business
    D. permanency

22. Missy has been paroled after serving 60 months of her 120-month prison sentence. Parole is effectively a release
    A. into the custody of a responsible person
    B. from incarceration after serving part of a sentence
    C. from incarceration after serving more than half or a majority of a sentence
    D. into the custody of a probation officer who will continue to monitor the individual indefinitely

23. A petitioner is also known as the _____ or the person starting the lawsuit.
    A. applicant
    B. plaintiff
    C. respondent
    D. defendant

24. After learning more about the circumstances surrounding the alleged armed robbery committed by Justin and three of his friends, the state's prosecutor decides to replace the original armed robbery charge against Justin for conspiracy to commit a felony.
    The prosecutor asks the court grant her request to enter a
    A. new charge
    B. substitute charge
    C. felonious charge
    D. determination of guilt

25. At a pretrial hearing to determine the credibility of the state's expert witness, the witness appeared and gave testimony followed by oral arguments by both the plaintiff's attorney and the defendant's attorney. Following the conference, each party decided they would like to review the record of what was said during that hearing prior to the trial. There was a stenographer during the pretrial hearing.
    Each party needs to request a(n)
    A. docket
    B. witness log
    C. transcript
    D. disclosure

KEY (CORRECT ANSWERS)

1.	C	11.	D
2.	C	12.	A
3.	B	13.	A
4.	D	14.	B
5.	A	15.	D
6.	B	16.	C
7.	A	17.	B
8.	A	18.	D
9.	C	19.	A
10.	B	20.	C

21. A
22. B
23. B
24. B
25. C

EXAMINATION SECTION
TEST 1

DIRECTIONS: Each question or incomplete statement is followed by several suggested answers or completions. Select the one that BEST answers the question or completes the statement. *PRINT THE LETTER OF THE CORRECT ANSWER IN THE SPACE AT THE RIGHT.*

Questions 1-5.

DIRECTIONS: Questions 1 through 5 are to be answered on the basis of the following fact pattern.

Astrid's son, Carlos, attends the local high school. Carlos and another student, Manny, have been bullying another student both on and off school premises. The high school principal has notified the New York Police Department School Safety Unit of the issue. The principal has also been in touch with Astrid and Manny's mother, Mary. Mary believes Carlos is a bad influence to her son, Manny. After obtaining Astrid's phone number, Mary called Astrid and made threats towards her and Carlos. She indicated that if Carlos did not stay away from her son, Manny, she would have them both killed. The next day after school, Carlos is jumped by a group of teenagers and his leg is broken in the brawl. Astrid sues Manny, Mary, and the school district. Mary intends to countersue.

1. Who is the complainant?
   A. Manny   B. Mary   C. Astrid   D. Carlos

2. Which of the following is NOT a possible cause of action?
   A. Harassment
   B. Assault
   C. Negligence
   D. Breach of Contract

3. What key information is missing from the complaint?
   A. The name of the bullied student
   B. The location where Carlos was jumped
   C. The name of the high school principal
   D. The name of the police officer at the NYPD School Safety Unit who was originally notified on the issue

4. Is Mary obligated to countersue because she or her son, Manny, may have been involved in the assault against Carlos?
   A. Yes; she must answer the suit and countersue as required
   B. Yes; she must countersue to clear her son's name
   C. No; Mary is not obligated to countersue and can simply answer to the claims as alleged
   D. No; Mary is not obligated to countersue but she is obligated to countersue on Manny's behalf

5. Assume that Carlos and Manny are minors. 5.____
   What effect, if any, would this fact have on the lawsuit that is filed?
   A. The legal guardians of Carlos and Manny will need to file, and answer, the lawsuit on their behalf.
   B. Carlos and Manny do not need to appear in court.
   C. Minors cannot sue other people.
   D. The lawsuit is unaffected by their age.

6. 6.____

Mary Williams 1 Court Way Smithtown, NY 10170	Mary S. Williams 1 Court Way Smithtown, NY 10170	Mary S. Williams 1 Court Way Smith Town, NY 10170

   Which selection below accurately describes the addresses as listed above?
   A. All three addresses are the same.
   B. The first and the third address are the same.
   C. None of the addresses are the same.
   D. The second and third address are the same.

Questions 7-9.

DIRECTIONS: Questions 7 through 9 are to be answered on the basis of the following table.

Schedule – Judge Presser		
Petitioner	**Respondent**	**Status**
Williams	Smith	Dismissed with prejudice
Jones	Johnson	Continued
Adams	Doe	Dismissed with prejudice
Ash	Link	Adjourned
Lam	Garcia	Settled

7. How many cases were adjourned? 7.____
   A. 3   B. 1   C. 4   D. 5

8. In how many cases were money damages awarded by the judge? 8.____
   A. 0   B. 3   C. 4   D. 5

9. How many cases will be heard again? 9.____
   A. 2   B. 1   C. 3   D. 5

10. A warrant for the arrest of Benjamin Lang. Lang lives in Suffolk County, New York. What is recorded on the warrant? 10.____
    Lang's
    A. venue   B. domicile
    C. jurisdiction   D. subject matter jurisdiction

Questions 11-13.

DIRECTIONS: Questions 11 through 13 are to be answered on the basis of the following table.

455888912	455888812	455888912	455888812
Civil Court	Civil Court	Civil Court	Civil Court
Contract	Contract	Contract	Contract
Pam L. Williams	Pam Williams	Pam Williams	Pam L. Williams

11. Which selection below accurately describes the case captions as listed above?
    A. All of the captions are the same.
    B. Caption 1 and Caption 3 are the same.
    C. Caption 2 and Caption 4 are the same.
    D. None of the captions are the same.

12. Which digit above is dissimilar in two of the above captions?
    A. The seventh digit
    B. The fifth digit
    C. The sixth digit
    D. The eighth digit

13. The notation "contract" in each caption above describes the _____ of the case.
    A. Cause of action
    B. Remedy at issue
    C. Order of the court
    D. Disposition

14. Melinda was seen stealing money from a car on Atlantic Avenue in Brooklyn. Samuel witnessed the crime from his apartment and called the police. Officer Tang recorded the call in the police log. Samuel does not own a car and reported the crime anonymously. Later that same evening, Jeremy returned his car and found the passenger window had been broken and $500 was stolen from the glove compartment. Jeremy called the police to report the crime.
    In the judge's docket, the petitioner of the case against Melinda is MOST likely
    A. Jeremy
    B. Samuel
    C. Officer Tang
    D. The petitioner is anonymous

15. Judge Oswald hears cases in the Surrogate Court.
    Which of the following would NOT be in Judge Oswald's court calendar?
    A. Adoption
    B. Wills
    C. Estate and Probation
    D. Negligence

Questions 16-19.

DIRECTIONS: Questions 16 through 19 are to be answered on the basis of the following fact pattern.

Judge Laredo, Smith and Ora hear no-fault cases in the 10th Judicial District throughout the week. Judge Laredo hears cases the first Monday of each month. Judge Smith hears cases with amounts in dispute over $10,000 on Tuesday, Wednesday, and Friday. Judge Ora hears cases without amounts in dispute below $25,000 on Tuesdays only.

16. Geico and ABC Chiropractic are parties to a no-fault dispute with an amount in dispute of $8,500.
    If Judge Laredo is unavailable, what day can the case be heard?
    A. Wednesday   B. Friday   C. Monday   D. Tuesday

17. Blue Health Medical and Progressive Insurance are parties to a no-fault dispute which is scheduled to be heard February 18th. Blue Health demands Progressive reimburse the provider $5,000 for the primary surgeon fees and $12,000 in assistant surgeon fees.
    Which judge will hear the matter and on which day?
    A. Judge Smith on Friday   B. Judge Smith on Tuesday
    C. Judge Smith on Wednesday   D. Judge Ora on Tuesday

18. A no-fault dispute is being heard on Monday, June 10th.
    Which statement below must be TRUE?
    A. The amount in dispute is above $10,000.
    B. The amount in dispute is less than $25,000.
    C. The amount in dispute is less than $10,000.
    D. Judge Laredo is hearing the case.

19. What information must be obtained in order to properly schedule the court calendar?
    A. The amount in dispute for each case
    B. The parties in each case
    C. Verification the dispute is "no-fault in nature"
    D. All of the above

20. A victim impact statement is an oral or _____ statement that may be read in court.
    A. recorded   B. transcribed   C. written   D. visualized

21. The clerk in the Surrogates Court will need to have access to what information in the preparation of adoption hearings?
    A. Personal information of a child's current or prior legal guardian
    B. Emancipation petition documentation
    C. Deed or will
    D. Probate documentation

Questions 22-25.

DIRECTIONS: Questions 22 through 25 are to be answered on the basis of the following table.

Schedule – Judge Orlando			
Complainant/Plaintiff	**Defendant**	**Case Type**	**Money Awarded**
Williams	Smith	Civil	$5,000
Jones	Johnson	Criminal	No
Adams	Doe	Criminal	$10,000
Ash	Link	Civil	$15,000
Lam	Garcia	Civil	$25,000

5 (#1)

22. What is the total amount of money damages from civil disputes?   22._____
    A. $45,000   B. $40,000   C. $5,000   D. 0

23. Which complainant/plaintiff was awarded less than $20,000?   23._____
    A. Williams, Adams, and Ash   B. Jones, Adams, and Ash
    C. Lam, Williams, and Jones   D. Jones, Adams, and Lam

24. How many criminal cases were heard by Judge Orlando?   24._____
    A. 4   B. 5   C. 2   D. 3

25. Which defendants are responsible for paying more than $10,000?   25._____
    A. Doe and Link   B. Link and Garcia
    C. John and Doe   D. Smith and Garcia

KEY (CORRECT ANSWERS)

1.	C		11.	D
2.	D		12.	A
3.	B		13.	A
4.	C		14.	A
5.	A		15.	D
6.	C		16.	D
7.	B		17.	D
8.	A		18.	D
9.	A		19.	D
10.	B		20.	C

21. A
22. A
23. A
24. C
25. B

TEST 2

DIRECTIONS: Each question or incomplete statement is followed by several suggested answers or completions. Select the one that BEST answers the question or completes the statement. *PRINT THE LETTER OF THE CORRECT ANSWER IN THE SPACE AT THE RIGHT.*

Questions 1-4.

DIRECTIONS: Questions 1 through 4 are to be answered on the basis of the following text.

After a lengthy trial with multiple ___1___, Jim was acquitted of armed robbery and conspiracy. On the other hand, his alleged partner, Bob, was ___2___ of armed robbery. The conspiracy charge was dropped against Bob since the 12-person ___3___ found he acted alone. Jim's attorney ___4___.

1. Fill in the blank for #1:
    A. witnesses   B. evidence   C. discretionary   D. turbulent

2. Fill in the blank for #2:
    A. guilty   B. convicted   C. indicted   D. surmised

3. Fill in the blank for #3:
    A. judge   B. spectator   C. jury   D. bailiff

4. Fill in the blank for #4:
    A. appealed   B. remanded   C. reversed   D. rescinded

Questions 5-10.

DIRECTIONS: Questions 5 through 10 are to be answered on the basis of the following table.

Court Schedule - Tuesday			
Judge	Total Cases	Cases Dismissed	Cases with Money Awarded
Presser	10	2	X
O'Dell	5	5	
Williams	6	6	
Sasha	8	7	X

5. How many cases were awarded money damages from Judge Presser's calendar?
    A. 2   B. 8   C. 6   D. 10

6. How many cases were awarded money damages from Judge Sasha's calendar?
    A. 8   B. 7   C. 1   D. 0

7. How many cases were dismissed on Tuesday? 7._____
   A. 11   B. 20   C. 7   D. 10

8. How many cases were awarded money damages on Tuesday? 8._____
   A. 9   B. 8   C. 1   D. 10

9. Which judge heard the MOST cases on Tuesday? 9._____
   A. Presser   B. O'Dell   C. Williams   D. Sasha

10. Which judge heard the LEAST cases on Tuesday? 10._____
    A. Presser   B. O'Dell   C. Willliams   D. Sasha

Questions 11-15.

DIRECTIONS: Questions 11 through 15 are to be answered on the basis of the following text.

Judge Smith hears adoption cases on Fridays. Judge Clark hears criminal cases every weekday except Tuesday in the New York City Criminal Court. Judge Clark hears felony criminal cases on Tuesday in Supreme Court. Judge Amy hears felony criminal cases on Thursday in Supreme Court.

11. Daniel is being charged with the murder of his cousin, Jerrell. 11._____
    Which judge can hear the case and on what day?
    A. Judge Smith on Friday   B. Judge Clark on Monday
    C. Judge Amy on Tuesday   D. Judge Clark on Tuesday

12. Jamal lives in Staten Island with his sister, Tisha, and Tisha's boyfriend, 12._____
    Hunter. Hunter and Jamal do not get along and one day last January, Hunter
    and Jamal were involved in a physical altercation. Hunter and Jamal both
    allege that the other assault and battered the other.
    Which judge can hear the case and on what day?
    A. Judge Clark on Tuesday   B. Judge Amy on Thursday
    C. Judge Smith on Friday   D. Judge Clark on Monday

13. Assuming the crime of assault and battery are not felonies, in which court 13._____
    will Jamal and Hunter's dispute be heard?
    A. Supreme Court   B. Surrogates Court
    C. New York City Criminal Court   D. Small Claims Court

14. Assume that Tisha and Hunter have a six-year-old daughter. 14._____
    If Hunter is incarcerated for his role in the physical altercation with Jamal,
    which court would have jurisdiction over Hunter's trial?
    A. Surrogates Court   B. New York City Criminal Court
    C. Bronx Housing Court   D. Richmond County Civil Court

15. What day of the week are the MOST cases heard between all three judges? 15._____
    A. Monday   B. Thursday   C. Tuesday   D. Friday

Questions 16-19.

DIRECTIONS: Questions 16 through 19 are to be answered on the basis of the following table.

Caption #1	Caption #2	Caption #3	Caption #4
Case 12-908	Case 12-909	Case 12-910	Case 12-911
Bronx Housing Court	Civil Court	Civil Court	Surrogates Court
Landlord/Tenant	Assault	Breach of Contract	Guardianship
ABC Property Mgmt v. Sam Smith	Jim Jones v. Sam Hunt	Terrell Williams v. Daniel Tang	In re: Jane Doe

16. Which caption above contains an INCORRECT cause of action?
    A. 1   B. 2   C. 3   D. 4

17. When were the cases in each of the captions above initiated?
    A. 2015
    B. 2016
    C. 2012
    D. Unable to determine based on the information provided

18. Which case caption above corresponds to a matter that will NOT have monetary damages awarded?
    A. 1   B. 2   C. 3   D. 4

19. Which case caption has a matter involving an institutional, rather than an individual, petitioner?
    A. 1   B. 2   C. 3   D. 4

20. A pro se litigant wants to initiate a lawsuit against his intrusive neighbor. Assuming the pro se litigant prevails, which form should be served against the neighbor after the judgment is entered?
    A. Notice of entry
    B. Notice of appeal
    C. Remand service
    D. Process discovery

21. A(n) _____ is a hearing for the purpose of determining the amount of damages sue on a claim. The clerk can enter the request on the judge's calendar after the opposing party has defaulted.
    A. imposition   B. inquest   C. tardy notice   D. reversal

22. After a judgment is entered, it becomes enforceable for a period of time. For real property, a transcript of _____ is filed with the County Clerk which makes the judgment enforceable for a period of ten years.
    A. enforcement
    B. judgment
    C. engagement
    D. affidavit

23. Sensitive information must be _____ before it becomes public record.
    A. retained   B. reposed   C. redacted   D. recanted

24. Service of process can be filed upon the individual or upon the _____. The affidavit of service will state the party that received the service.
    A. secretary of state
    B. guardian
    C. ad litem
    D. second most suitable person

25. A warrant can be issued to a sheriff or a marshal. The warrant clerk is responsible for reviewing the paperwork and ensuring that all is in order, including
    A. the names of the parties
    B. address of the premises
    C. the index number
    D. all of the above

KEY (CORRECT ANSWERS)

1.	A		11.	D
2.	B		12.	D
3.	C		13.	C
4.	A		14.	B
5.	B		15.	D
6.	C		16.	B
7.	B		17.	C
8.	A		18.	D
9.	A		19.	A
10.	B		20.	A

21. B
22. B
23. C
24. A
25. D

TEST 3

DIRECTIONS: Each question or incomplete statement is followed by several suggested answers or completions. Select the one that BEST answers the question or completes the statement. *PRINT THE LETTER OF THE CORRECT ANSWER IN THE SPACE AT THE RIGHT.*

1. Supreme Court clerks need to be on notice when a(n) _____ is filed as a judge is not assigned until one that parties files this document and pays the filing fee. A case will never go to trial if this document is never filed.
   A. request for maintenance
   B. request for judicial intervention
   C. remediation
   D. arbitration

   1._____

Questions 2-4.

DIRECTIONS: Questions 1 through 5 are to be answered on the basis of the following chart.

Row	Case Type	Court
1	Divorce	Supreme Court
2	Custody/Visitation	Family Court
3	Child Support	Family Court
4	Paternity	Family Court
5	When Someone Dies	Surrogates Court
6	Guardianship	Surrogate's Court
7	Name Change	Supreme Court
8	Housing	New York City Housing Court

2. Assume that you are advising a pro se litigant on the proper forms to file when representing him or herself. Where would John file a small estate affidavit?
   A. Family Court
   B. Supreme Court
   C. Surrogates Court
   D. New York Civil Court

   2._____

3. Where would Tom's sister, Emmanuela, file a name change?
   A. Supreme Court
   B. Family Court
   C. Surrogates Court
   D. New York City Civil Court

   3._____

4. Tara and her husband, Cassidy, share custody of their twin sons, Drake and Austin. Cassidy would like to petition the court for sole custody. Where would Cassidy file his petition?
   A. New York City Housing Court
   B. Supreme Court
   C. Family Court
   D. Surrogates Court

   4._____

5. Richard is representing himself in a lawsuit against his landlord. Richard does not have the financial means to hire an attorney and would like to request a reduction in the court filing fees. Richard must file a request for a _____ which is made by filing a _____ and sworn _____ which explains his finances to the court.
   A. fee waiver; notice of motion; affirmation
   B. fee waiver, notice of motion, affidavit
   C. affidavit, notice of motion, fee waiver
   D. affidavit, fee waiver, notice of motion

Questions 6-10.

DIRECTIONS: Questions 6 through 10 are to be answered on the basis of the following text.

Daniel walks into this local supermarket after lunch and falls in one of the store aisles. Daniel lies on the floor – which is nearly empty – until one of the store managers finds him, helps him up, and offers to pay for his groceries. Daniel leaves the store bruised, but not seriously injured. Two days later, Daniel falls at another grocery store. This time, Daniel threatens to sue the grocery store. The second grocery store has heard about Daniel and is concerned that he is falsifying his injuries to gain sympathy and money. The second grocery store sues Daniel to get ahead of Daniel suing them.

6. Who is the plaintiff in the case?
   A. The first grocery store
   B. The second grocery store
   C. The grocery store manager
   D. Daniel

7. Which of the following is the MOST likely cause of action in a suit that Daniel initiates against the grocery store?
   A. Breach of contract
   B. Discrimination
   C. Negligence
   D. Assault

8. After the lawsuit has commenced, which party would respond or file an answer to the complaint?
   A. Daniel
   B. The first grocery store
   C. The second grocery store
   D. The grocery store manager

9. Which party is eligible to countersue?
   A. The first grocery store
   B. The second grocery store
   C. The grocery store manager
   D. Daniel

10. The lawsuit will likely be dismissed. Why?
    A. Daniel is clearly not exaggerating his injuries.
    B. Daniel has not sued either grocery store.
    C. The store manager did not take a report of Daniel's injuries.
    D. The first grocery store must sue Daniel first.

11. A settlement between parties is not a final and binding legal agreement until the _____ of settlement is signed by both parties.
    A. amendment   B. agreement   C. stipulation   D. simulation

12. Which of the following are appropriate reasons for filing an Order to Show Cause?
    A. Changing the terms of a court order
    B. Requesting the court to dismiss a case
    C. Bringing the case back to court for any reason
    D. All of the above

12._____

13. Which of the following is NOT an appropriate reason for filing an Order to Show Case?
    A. Asking for more time to do something previously agreed upon by court order
    B. Explaining why either party missed a court date
    C. Submitting financial information for a landlord/tenant dispute
    D. Fixing errors in a stipulation

13._____

Questions 14-17.

DIRECTIONS: Questions 14 through 17 are to be answered on the basis of the following text.

Judge Chin hears child neglect and abuse cases in Family Court on Mondays and Tuesdays. Judge Amy hears divorce cases on Mondays, Wednesdays, and Fridays. Judge Snell hears child support and visitation cases every day of the week except Thursday. Termination of parental rights, foster care placement, and other child support cases are scheduled on Thursdays only with any of the three judges.

14. Tim and Sarah would like to adjust their visitation schedule for their eight-year-old daughter, Samantha. They would like the courts to assist them with this issue as they have been unable to come to an agreement on their own.
    Which judge will hear the case and on what day?
    A. Judge Snell on Thursday
    B. Judge Snell on Monday
    C. Judge Chin on Monday
    D. Judge Chin on Friday

14._____

15. Amanda would like to file for emancipation from her parents.
    Which judge is MOST likely to hear her case?
    A. Judge Chin
    B. Judge Amy
    C. Judge Snell'
    D. Any of the judges can hear Amanda's case

15._____

16. Jimmy and Eva are legally separating. Which judge will hear their case and on what day?
    A. Judge Chin on Monday
    B. Judge Snell on Monday
    C. Judge Amy on Monday
    D. Judge Chin on Tuesday

16._____

17. The State of New York intends to file a case against Eric for the abuses and neglect of his daughter, Clare. Eric, however, is not Clare's legal guardian. Clare's legal guardian is her grandmother, Allison. Even though it is not clear that Clare has been neglected, the courts have found that Clare should be placed into foster care until it can be determined who the ultimate caregiver should be.
Which judge will MOST likely hear this case?
    A. Judge Amy
    B. Judge Chin
    C. Judge Snell
    D. Any of the judges can hear this case

Questions 18-25.

DIRECTIONS: Questions 18 through 25 are to be answered on the basis of the following chart.

Item	Fee
Obtaining an index number	$210
RJI	$95
Note of Issue	$30
Motion or Cross-Motion	$45
Demand for Jury Trial	$65
Voluntary Discontinuance	$35
Notice of Appeal	$65

18. What is the final cost to obtain an index number, demand a jury trial, and file a notice of appeal?
    A. $210 B. $35 C. $65 D. $310

19. What is the final cost to obtain an RJI and note of issue?
    A. $125 B. $95 C. $30 D. $65

20. Which of the following is MOST likely to be filed with an RJI?
    A. Demand for jury trial
    B. Notice of appeal
    C. Voluntary discontinuance
    D. Obtaining an index number

21. Which of the following is the MOST likely outcome of filing a voluntary discontinuance?
The case
    A. is automatically appealed
    B. is dismissed
    C. is rescheduled
    D. will be remanded

22. What is the final cost of filing a notice of appeal?
    A. $35 B. $65 C. $95 D. $120

23. What is the final cost of all items prior to filing a motion or cross-motion?
    A. $210 B. $95 C. $45 D. $335

24. Jamal would like to petition the court to compel discovery from his adversary and former friend, Bob. He would also like to speed up the date of trial by filing a demand for jury trial and RJI.
What is the final cost to do so?
   A. $160   B. $95   C. $65   D. $205

25. What is the LEAST costly court document filing fee?
   A. Notice of motion
   B. Demand for jury trial
   C. Note of issue
   D. RJI

KEY (CORRECT ANSWERS)

1.	B	11.	C
2.	C	12.	D
3.	A	13.	C
4.	C	14.	B
5.	B	15.	D
6.	B	16.	C
7.	C	17.	D
8.	A	18.	D
9.	D	19.	A
10.	B	20.	D

21. B
22. B
23. D
24. D
25. C

TEST 4

DIRECTIONS: Each question or incomplete statement is followed by several suggested answers or completions. Select the one that BEST answers the question or completes the statement. *PRINT THE LETTER OF THE CORRECT ANSWER IN THE SPACE AT THE RIGHT.*

1. A lawsuit for money damages amounting to more than $25,000 can be heard in which court? 1.____
   A. Surrogates Court
   B. Supreme Court
   C. New York City Civil Court
   D. New York City Criminal Court

2. Which of the following will NOT be on a Notice of Entry? 2.____
   A. Name of plaintiff
   B. Name of defendant
   C. Index number
   D. Social Security number

3. Court clerks are prohibited from which of the following? 3.____
   A. Predicting the judgment of the court
   B. Explaining available options for a case or problem
   C. Providing past rulings
   D. Providing citations or copies of the law

4. Court clerks are permitted to do all of the following EXCEPT 4.____
   A. provide forms with instructions
   B. instruct an individual on how to make a complaint
   C. analyze the law based on the specifics of a case
   D. describe court records and their availability

5. Mary would like to sue her neighbor, Jacob, for money damages. Mary claims Jacob ran his car into Mary's garage door while it was down and caused $5,000 in damages. For claims below $1,000, the filing fee is $15, while the filing fee is $5 more for claims above $1,000.
   How much is Mary's filing fee? 5.____
   A. $15   B. $10   C. $20   D. $25

Questions 6-10.

DIRECTIONS: Questions 6 through 10 are to be answered on the basis of the following table.

Schedule – Judge O'Neill		
Wednesday	**Thursday**	**Friday**
Continued	Dismissed with prejudice	Dismissed with prejudice
Continued	Adjourned	Continued
Settled	Dismissed with prejudice	Dismissed without prejudice
Settled	Continued	Settled
Settled	Continued	Settled

6. How many cases were adjourned this week? 6.____
   A. 5   B. 6   C. 1   D. 2

7. How many cases settled this week?
   A. 5   B. 4   C. 3   D. 8

8. How many cases were dismissed this week?
   A. 6   B. 4   C. 5   D. 7

9. How many cases will likely be heard again or, in other words, how many cases can be re-filed or are otherwise continued?
   A. 6   B. 5   C. 7   D. 8

10. Which day was Judge O'Neill the LEAST busy?
    A. Thursday
    B. Friday
    C. Wednesday
    D. Each day was equally busy

Questions 11-15.

DIRECTIONS: Questions 11 through 15 are to be answered on the basis of the following text.

At Alex's arraignment, he pled ___1___ to the charge of driving under the influence and vehicular manslaughter. At trial, the prosecutor presented evidence from several ___2___ that testified Alex had a drinking problem. While Alex's defense attorneys ___3___ to that testimony and argued it was hearsay, the judge overruled those objections and allowed the testimony to be entered in the record as originally spoken. At the conclusion of the trial, Alex was found ___4___ and sentenced to community service.

11. Fill in the blank for #1:
    A. nolo   B. contendere   C. not guilty   D. guilty

12. Fill in the blank for #2:
    A. witnesses   B. evidence   C. testimony   D. bearer

13. Fill in the blank for #3:
    A. disagreed   B. objected   C. qualified   D. disclaimed

14. Fill in the blank for #4:
    A. arraigned   B. protested   C. remanded   D. guilty

15. An acquittal can also be recorded in court documentation as a finding of
    A. reversal   B. recusal   C. not guilty   D. remand

16. Evidence must be found _____ before it can be marked and evaluated by the fact finder, either a judge or jury, in civil and criminal cases.
    A. relevant   B. redacted   C. qualified   D. admissible

17. The party who seeks an appeal from a decision of a court is deemed a(n) _____ and is recorded in court documentation as such.
    A. petitioner   B. respondent   C. appellant   D. re-respondent

18. How would a condominium be recorded in a bankruptcy proceeding?
    A. Real property
    B. Personal property
    C. Intangible asset
    D. chattel

19. Which of the following is LEAST likely to be recorded as a written statement describing one's legal and factual arguments?
    A. Attorney's brief
    B. Motion
    C. Summons
    D. Complaint

20. A lawsuit where one or more members of a large group of individuals sues on behalf of the other individuals in the large group is recorded as a _____ lawsuit.
    A. introductory
    B. class action
    C. municipality
    D. winning

21. Jamal has filed for bankruptcy. After the trustee has reviewed Jamal's assets, the trustee proposes a plan to the court where Jamal promises property that he already owns to satisfy the major of his debt.
    The property Jamal owns that will satisfy the debt is recorded as
    A. demerits
    B. collateral
    C. debris
    D. probate

22. Judge Presser has rendered Emilio's sentence for the charges of armed robbery and kidnapping. Emilio will serve 10 years for armed robbery and 12 years for kidnapping.
    If Emilio's total time in prison is 12 years, his sentence is recorded as
    A. consecutive
    B. demonstrative
    C. concurrent
    D. rebated

23. Assume the same facts as the previous question, but assume Emilio serves 22 years in prison.
    In this instance, his sentence is recorded as
    A. consecutive
    B. demonstrative
    C. concurrent
    D. rebated

24. A conviction can also be recorded in court records as a judgment of _____ against a defendant.
    A. guilt
    B. remorse
    C. retaliation
    D. acquittal

25. In bankruptcy, Jamal sells his house to his mother for $5 in an effort to hide it from creditors who will require that he sell it to satisfy his debts.
    This sale is recorded as a
    A. fraudulent transfer
    B. falsified sale
    C. remarkable trade
    D. clawback trade

KEY (CORRECT ANSWERS)

1.	B	11.	C
2.	D	12.	A
3.	A	13.	B
4.	C	14.	D
5.	C	15.	C
6.	C	16.	D
7.	A	17.	C
8.	B	18.	A
9.	A	19.	C
10.	C	20.	B

21.	B
22.	C
23.	A
24.	A
25.	A

RECORD KEEPING
EXAMINATION SECTION
TEST 1

DIRECTIONS: Each question or incomplete statement is followed by several suggested answers or completions. Select the one that BEST answers the question or completes the statement. *PRINT THE LETTER OF THE CORRECT ANSWER IN THE SPACE AT THE RIGHT.*

Questions 1-7.

DIRECTIONS: In answering Questions 1 through 7, use the following master list. For each question, determine where the name would fit on the master list. Each answer choice indicates right before or after the name in the answer choice.

    Aaron, Jane
    Armstead, Brendan
    Bailey, Charles
    Dent, Ricardo
    Grant, Mark
    Mars, Justin
    Methieu, Justine
    Parker, Cathy
    Sampson, Suzy
    Thomas, Heather

1. Schmidt, William
   A. Right before Cathy Parker
   B. Right after Heather Thomas
   C. Right after Suzy Sampson
   D. Right before Ricardo Dent

1.____

2. Asanti, Kendall
   A. Right before Jane Aaron
   B. Right after Charles Bailey
   C. Right before Justine Methieu
   D. Right after Brendan Armstead

2.____

3. O'Brien, Daniel
   A. Right after Justine Methieu
   B. Right before Jane Aaron
   C. Right after Mark Grant
   D. Right before Suzy Sampson

3.____

4. Marrow, Alison
   A. Right before Cathy Parker
   B. Right before Justin Mars
   C. Right before Mark Grant
   D. Right after Heather Thomas

4.____

5. Grantt, Marissa
   A. Right before Mark Grant
   B. Right after Mark Grant
   C. Right after Justin Mars
   D. Right before Suzy Sampson

5.____

6. Thompson, Heath 6.____
   A. Right after Justin Mars
   B. Right before Suzy Sampson
   C. Right after Heather Thomas
   D. Right before Cathy Parker

DIRECTIONS: Before answering Question 7, add in all of the names from Questions 1 through 6. Then fit the name in alphabetical order based on the new list.

7. Francisco, Mildred 7.____
   A. Right before Mark Grant
   B. Right after Marissa Grantt
   C. Right before Alison Marrow
   D. Right after Kendall Asanti

Questions 8-10.

DIRECTIONS: In answering Questions 8 through 10, compare each pair of names and addresses. Indicate whether they are the same or different in any way.

8. William H. Pratt, J.D.   William H. Pratt, J.D. 8.____
   Attourney at Law   Attorney at Law
   A. No differences   B. 1 difference
   C. 2 differences   D. 3 differences

9. 1303 Theater Drive,; Apt. 3-B   1330 Theatre Drive,; Apt. 3-B 9.____
   A. No differences   B. 1 difference
   C. 2 differences   D. 3 differences

10. Petersdorff, Briana and Mary   Petersdorff, Briana and Mary 10.____
    A. No differences   B. 1 difference
    C. 2 differences   D. 3 differences

11. Which of the following words, if any, are misspelled? 11.____
    A. Affordable
    B. Circumstansial
    C. Legalese
    D. None of the above

Questions 12-13.

DIRECTIONS: Questions 12 and 13 are to be answered on the basis of the following table.

Standardized Test Results for High School Students in District #1230

	English	Math	Science	Reading
High School 1	21	22	15	18
High School 2	12	16	13	15
High School 3	16	18	21	17
High School 4	19	14	15	16

The scores for each high school in the district were averaged out and listed for each subject tested. Scores of 0-10 are significantly below College Readiness Standards. 11-15 are below College Readiness, 16-20 meet College Readiness, and 21-25 are above College Readiness.

12. If the high schools need to meet or exceed in at least half the categories in order to NOT be considered "at risk," which schools are considered "at risk"? 12.____
    A. High School 2
    B. High School 3
    C. High School 4
    D. Both A and C

13. What percentage of subjects did the district as a whole meet or exceed College Readiness standards? 13.____
    A. 25%   B. 50%   C. 75%   D. 100%

Questions 14-15.

DIRECTIONS: Questions 14 and 15 are to be answered on the basis of the following information.

You have seven employees working as a part of your team: Austin, Emily, Jeremy, Christina, Martin, Harriet, and Steve. You have just sent an e-mail informing them that there will be a mandatory training session next week. To ensure that work still gets done, you are offering the training twice during the week: once on Tuesday and also on Thursday. This way half the employees will still be working while the other half attend the training. The only other issue is that Jeremy doesn't work on Tuesdays and Harriet doesn't work on Thursdays due to compressed work schedules.

14. Which of the following is a possible attendance roster for the first training session? 14.____
    A. Emily, Jeremy, Steve
    B. Steve, Christina, Harriet
    C. Harriet, Jeremy, Austin
    D. Steve, Martin, Jeremy

15. If Harriet, Christina, and Steve attend the training session on Tuesday, which of the following is a possible roster for Thursday's training session? 15.____
    A. Jeremy, Emily, and Austin
    B. Emily, Martin, and Harriet
    C. Austin, Christina, and Emily
    D. Jeremy, Emily, and Steve

Questions 16-20.

DIRECTIONS: In answering Questions 16 through 20, you will be given a word and will need to choose the answer choice that is MOST similar or different to the word.

16. Which word means the SAME as *annual*? 16.____
    A. Monthly   B. Usually   C. Yearly   D. Constantly

17. Which word means the SAME as *effort*? 17.____
    A. Energy   B. Equate   C. Cherish   D. Commence

18. Which word means the OPPOSITE of *forlorn*? 18.____
    A. Neglected   B. Lethargy   C. Optimistic   D. Astonished

19. Which word means the SAME as *risk*? 19.____
    A. Admire   B. Hazard   C. Limit   D. Hesitant

4 (#1)

20. Which word means the OPPOSITE of *translucent*? 20.____
    A. Opaque   B. Transparent   C. Luminous   D. Introverted

21. Last year, Jamie's annual salary was $50,000. Her boss called her today to inform her that she would receive a 20% raise for the upcoming year. How much more money will Jamie receive next year? 21.____
    A. $60,000   B. $10,000   C. $1,000   D. $51,000

22. You and a co-worker work for a temp hiring agency as part of their office staff. You both are given 6 days off per month. How many days off are you and your co-worker given in a year? 22.____
    A. 24   B. 72   C. 144   D. 48

23. If Margot makes $34,000 per year and she works 40 hours per week for all 52 weeks, what is her hourly rate? 23.____
    A. $16.34/hour   B. $17.00/hour   C. $15.54/hour   D. $13.23/hour

24. How many dimes are there in $175.00? 24.____
    A. 175   B. 1,750   C. 3,500   D. 17,500

25. If Janey is three times as old as Emily, and Emily is 3, how old is Janey? 25.____
    A. 6   B. 9   C. 12   D. 15

KEY (CORRECT ANSWERS)

1.	C	11.	B
2.	D	12.	A
3.	A	13.	D
4.	B	14.	B
5.	B	15.	A
6.	C	16.	C
7.	A	17.	A
8.	B	18.	C
9.	C	19.	B
10.	A	20.	A

21.	B
22.	C
23.	A
24.	B
25.	B

TEST 2

DIRECTIONS: Each question or incomplete statement is followed by several suggested answers or completions. Select the one that BEST answers the question or completes the statement. *PRINT THE LETTER OF THE CORRECT ANSWER IN THE SPACE AT THE RIGHT.*

Questions 1-6.

DIRECTIONS: Questions 1 through 6 are to be answered on the basis of the following information.

item	name of item to be ordered
quantity	minimum number that can be ordered
beginning amount	amount in stock at start of month
amount received	amount receiving during month
ending amount	amount in stock at end of month
amount used	amount used during month
amount to order	will need at least as much of each item as used in the previous month
unit price	cost of each unit of an item
total price	total price for the order

Item	Quantity	Beginning	Received	Ending	Amount Used	Amount to Order	Unit Price	Total Price
Pens	10	22	10	8	24	20	$0.11	$2.20
Spiral notebooks	8	30	13	12			$0.25	
Binder clips	2 boxes	3 boxes	1 box	1 box			$1.79	
Sticky notes	3 packs	12 packs	4 packs	2 packs			$1.29	
Dry erase markers	1 pack (dozen)	34 markers	8 markers	40 markers			$16.49	
Ink cartridges (printer)	1 cartridge	3 cartridges	1 cartridge	2 cartridges			$79.99	
Folders	10 folders	25 folders	15 folders	10 folders			$1.08	

1. How many packs of sticky notes were used during the month?   1.____
   A. 16   B. 10   C. 12   D. 14

2. How many folders need to be ordered for next month?   2.____
   A. 15   B. 20   C. 30   D. 40

3. What is the total price of notebooks that you will need to order?   3.____
   A. $6.00   B. $0.25   C. $4.50   D. $2.75

4. Which of the following will you spend the second most money on?   4.____
   A. Ink cartridges   B. Dry erase markers
   C. Sticky notes   D. Binder clips

5. How many packs of dry erase markers should you order?   5.____
   A. 1   B. 8   C. 12   D. 0

53

6. What will be the total price of the file folders you order?
   A. $20.16   B. $21.60   C. $10.80   D. $4.32

Questions 7-11.

DIRECTIONS: Questions 7 through 11 are to be answered on the basis of the following table.

Number of Car Accidents, By Location and Cause, for 2014						
	Location 1		Location 2		Location 3	
Cause	Number	Percent	Number	Percent	Number	Percent
Severe Weather	10		25		30	
Excessive Speeding	20	40	5		10	
Impaired Driving	15		15	25	8	
Miscellaneous	5		15		2	4
TOTALS	50	100	60	100	50	100

7. Which of the following is the third highest cause of accidents for all three locations?
   A. Severe Weather   B. Impaired Driving
   C. Miscellaneous   D. Excessive Speeding

8. The average number of Severe Weather accidents per week at Location 3 for the year (52 weeks) was MOST NEARLY
   A. 0.57   B. 30   C. 1   D. 1.25

9. Which location had the LARGEST percentage of accidents caused by Impaired Driving?
   A. 1   B. 2   C. 3   D. Both A and B

10. If one-third of the accidents at all three locations resulted in at least one fatality, what is the LEAST amount of deaths caused by accidents last year?
    A. 60   B. 106   C. 66   D. 53

11. What is the percentage of accidents caused by miscellaneous means from all three locations in 2014?
    A. 5%   B. 10%   C. 13%   D. 25%

12. How many pairs of the following groups of letters are exactly alike?

    ACDOBJ   ACDBOJ
    HEWBWR   HEWRWB
    DEERVS   DEERVS
    BRFQSX   BRFQSX
    WEYRVB   WEYRVB
    SPQRZA   SQRPZA

    A. 2   B. 3   C. 4   D. 5

Questions 13-19.

DIRECTIONS: Questions 13 through 19 are to be answered on the basis of the following information.

In 2012, the most current information on the American population was finished. The information was compiled by 200 volunteers in each of the 50 states. The territory of Puerto Rico, a sovereign of the United States, had 25 people assigned to compile data. In February of 2010, volunteers in each state and sovereign began collecting information. In Puerto Rico, data collection finished by January 31st, 2011, while work in the United States was completed on June 30, 2012. Each volunteer gathered data on the population of their state or sovereign. When the information was compiled, volunteers sent reports to the nation's capital, Washington, D.C. Each volunteer worked 20 hours per month and put together 10 reports per month. After the data was compiled in total, 50 people reviewed the data and worked from January 2012 to December 2012.

13. How many reports were generated from February 2010 to April 2010 in Illinois and Ohio?
    A. 3,000   B. 6,000   C. 12,000   D. 15,000

14. How many volunteers in total collected population data in January 2012?
    A. 10,000   B. 2,000   C. 225   D. 200

15. How many reports were put together in May 2012?
    A. 2,000   B. 50,000   C. 100,000   D. 100,250

16. How many hours did the Puerto Rican volunteers work in the fall (September-November)?
    A. 60   B. 500   C. 1,500   D. 0

17. How many workers were compiling or reviewing data in July 2012?
    A. 25   B. 50   C. 200   D. 250

18. What was the total amount of hours worked by Nevada volunteers in July 2010?
    A. 500   B. 4,000   C. 4,500   D. 5,000

19. How many reviewers worked in January 2013?
    A. 75   B. 50   C. 0   D. 25

20. John has to file 10 documents per shelf. How many documents would it take for John to fill 40 shelves?
    A. 40   B. 400   C. 4,500   D. 5,000

21. Jill wants to travel from New York City to Los Angeles by bike, which is approximately 2,772 miles. How many miles per day would Jill need to average if she wanted to complete the trip in 4 weeks?
    A. 100   B. 89   C. 99   D. 94

22. If there are 24 CPU's and only 7 monitors, how many more monitors do you need to have the same amount of monitors as CPU's?
    A. Not enough information
    B. 17
    C. 31
    D. 0

    22.____

23. If Gerry works 5 days a week and 8 hours each day, and John works 3 days a week and 10 hours each day, how many more hours per year will Gerry work than John?
    A. They work the same amount of hours.
    B. 450
    C. 520
    D. 832

    23.____

24. Jimmy gets transferred to a new office. The new office has 25 employees, but only 16 are there due to a blizzard. How many coworkers was Jimmy able to meet on his first day?
    A. 16   B. 25   C. 9   D. 7

    24.____

25. If you do a fundraiser for charities in your area and raise $500 total, how much would you give to each charity if you were donating equal amounts to 3 of them?
    A. $250.00   B. $167.77   C. $50.00   D. $111.11

    25.____

KEY (CORRECT ANSWERS)

1.	D		11.	C
2.	B		12.	B
3.	A		13.	C
4.	C		14.	A
5.	D		15.	C
6.	B		16.	C
7.	D		17.	B
8.	A		18.	B
9.	A		19.	C
10.	D		20.	B

21. C
22. B
23. C
24. A
25. B

TEST 3

DIRECTIONS: Each question or incomplete statement is followed by several suggested answers or completions. Select the one that BEST answers the question or completes the statement. *PRINT THE LETTER OF THE CORRECT ANSWER IN THE SPACE AT THE RIGHT.*

Questions 1-3.

DIRECTIONS: In answering Questions 1 through 3, choose the correctly spelled word.

1. A. allusion B. alusion C. allusien D. allution 1.____
2. A. altitude B. alltitude C. atlitude D. altlitude 2.____
3. A. althogh B. allthough C. althrough D. although 3.____

Questions 4-9.

DIRECTIONS: In answering Questions 4 through 9, choose the answer that BEST completes the analogy.

4. Odometer is to mileage as compass is to 4.____
   A. speed B. needle C. hiking D. direction

5. Marathon is to race as hibernation is to 5.____
   A. winter B. dream C. sleep D. bear

6. Cup is to coffee as bowl is to 6.____
   A. dish B. spoon C. food D. soup

7. Flow is to river as stagnant is to 7.____
   A. pool B. rain C. stream D. canal

8. Paw is to cat as hoof is to 8.____
   A. lamb B. horse C. lion D. elephant

9. Architect is to building as sculptor is to 9.____
   A. museum B. chisel C. stone D. statue

Questions 10-14.

DIRECTIONS: Questions 10 through 14 are to be answered on the basis of the following graph.

Population of Carroll City Broken Down by Age and Gender (in Thousands)			
Age	Female	Male	Total
Under 15	60	60	120
15-23		22	
24-33		20	44
34-43	13	18	31
44-53	20		67
64 and Over	65	65	130
TOTAL	230	232	462

10. How many people in the city are between the ages of 15-23?
    A. 70 B. 46,000 C. 70,000 D. 225,000

11. Approximately what percentage of the total population of the city was female aged 24-33?
    A. 10% B. 5% C. 15% D. 25%

12. If 33% of the males have a job and 55% of females don't have a job, which of the following statements is TRUE?
    A. Males have approximately 2,600 more jobs than females.
    B. Females have approximately 49,000 more jobs than males.
    C. Females have approximately 26,000 more jobs than males.
    D. None of the above statements are true.

13. How many females between the ages of 15-23 live in Carroll City?
    A. 67,000 B. 24,000 C. 48,000 D. 91,000

14. Assume all males 44-53 living in Carroll City are employed. If two-thirds of males age 44-53 work jobs outside of Carroll City, how many work within city limits?
    A. 31,333
    B. 15,667
    C. 47,000
    D. Cannot answer the question with the information provided

10._____

11._____

12._____

13._____

14._____

Questions 15-16.

DIRECTIONS: Questions 15 and 16 are labeled as shown. Alphabetize them for filing. Choose the answer that correctly shows the order.

15. (1) AED
    (2) OOS
    (3) FOA
    (4) DOM
    (5) COB

    A. 2-5-4-3-2 B. 1-4-5-2-3 C. 1-5-4-2-3 D. 1-5-4-3-2

15.____

16. Alphabetize the names of the people. Last names are given last.
    (1) Lindsey Jamestown
    (2) Jane Alberta
    (3) Ally Jamestown
    (4) Allison Johnston
    (5) Lyle Moreno

    A. 2-1-3-4-5 B. 3-4-2-1-5 C. 2-3-1-4-5 D. 4-3-2-1-5

16.____

17. Which of the following words is misspelled?
    A. disgust   B. whisper
    C. locale   D. none of the above

17.____

Questions 18-21.

DIRECTIONS: Questions 18 through 21 are to be answered on the basis of the following list of employees.

    Robertson, Aaron
    Bacon, Gina
    Jerimiah, Trace
    Gillette, Stanley
    Jacks, Sharon

18. Which employee name would come in third in alphabetized list?
    A. Robertson, Aaron   B. Jerimiah, Trace
    C. Gillette, Stanley   D. Jacks, Sharon

18.____

19. Which employee's first name starts with the letter in the alphabet that is five letters after the first letter of their last name?
    A. Jerimiah, Trace   B. Bacon, Gina
    C. Jacks, Sharon   D. Gillette, Stanley

19.____

20. How many employees have last names that are exactly five letters long?
    A. 1   B. 2   C. 3   D. 4

20.____

21. How many of the employees have either a first or last name that starts   21._____
    with the letter "G"?
    A. 1   B. 2   C. 4   D. 5

Questions 22-25.

DIRECTIONS: Questions 22 through 25 are to be answered on the basis of the following chart.

Bicycle Sales (Model #34JA32)							
Country	May	June	July	August	September	October	Total
Germany	34	47	45	54	56	60	296
Britain	40	44	36	47	47	46	260
Ireland	37	32	32	32	34	33	200
Portugal	14	14	14	16	17	14	89
Italy	29	29	28	31	29	31	177
Belgium	22	24	24	26	25	23	144
Total	176	198	179	206	208	207	1166

22. What percentage of the overall total was sold to the German importer?   22._____
    A. 25.3%   B. 22%   C. 24.1%   D. 23%

23. What percentage of the overall total was sold in September?   23._____
    A. 24.1%   B. 25.6%   C. 17.9%   D. 24.6%

24. What is the average number of units per month imported into Belgium over   24._____
    the first four months shown?
    A. 26   B. 20   C. 24   D. 31

25. If you look at the three smallest importers, what is their total import   25._____
    percentage?
    A. 35.1%   B. 37.1%   C. 40%   D. 28%

KEY (CORRECT ANSWERS)

1. A
2. A
3. D
4. D
5. C

6. D
7. A
8. B
9. D
10. C

11. B
12. C
13. C
14. B
15. D

16. C
17. D
18. D
19. B
20. B

21. B
22. A
23. C
24. C
25. A

TEST 4

DIRECTIONS: Each question or incomplete statement is followed by several suggested answers or completions. Select the one that BEST answers the question or completes the statement. *PRINT THE LETTER OF THE CORRECT ANSWER IN THE SPACE AT THE RIGHT.*

Questions 1-6.

DIRECTIONS: In answering Questions 1 through 6, choose the sentence that represents the BEST example of English grammar.

1. A. Joey and me want to go on a vacation next week. 1.____
   B. Gary told Jim he would need to take some time off.
   C. If turning six years old, Jim's uncle would teach Spanish to him.
   D. Fax a copy of your resume to Ms. Perez and me.

2. A. Jerry stood in line for almost two hours. 2.____
   B. The reaction to my engagement was less exciting than I thought it would be.
   C. Carlos and me have done great work on this project.
   D. Two parts of the speech needs to be revised before tomorrow.

3. A. Arriving home, the alarm was tripped. 3.____
   B. Jonny is regarded as a stand up guy, a responsible parent, and he doesn't give up until a task is finished.
   C. Each employee must submit a drug test each month.
   D. One of the documents was incinerated in the explosion.

4. A. As soon as my parents get home, I told them I finished all of my chores. 4.____
   B. I asked my teacher to send me my missing work, check my absences, and how did I do on my test.
   C. Matt attempted to keep it concealed from Jenny and me.
   D. If Mary or him cannot get work done on time, I will have to split them up.

5. A. Driving to work, the traffic report warned him of an accident on Highway 47. 5.____
   B. Jimmy has performed well this season.
   C. Since finishing her degree, several job offers have been given to Cam.
   D. Our boss is creating unstable conditions for we employees.

6. A. The thief was described as a tall man with a wiry mustache weighing approximately 150 pounds. 6.____
   B. She gave Patrick and I some more time to finish our work.
   C. One of the books that he ordered was damaged in shipping.
   D. While talking on the rotary phone, the car Jim was driving skidded off the road.

Questions 7-9.

DIRECTIONS: Questions 7 through 9 are to be answered on the basis of the following graph.

Ice Lake Frozen Flight (2002-2013)		
Year	Number of Participants	Temperature (Fahrenheit)
2002	22	4°
2003	50	33°
2004	69	18°
2005	104	22°
2006	108	24°
2007	288	33°
2008	173	9°
2009	598	39°
2010	698	26°
2011	696	30°
2012	777	28°
2013	578	32°

7. Which two year span had the LARGEST difference between temperatures?
   A. 2002 and 2003
   B. 2011 and 2012
   C. 2008 and 2009
   D. 2003 and 2004

8. How many total people participated in the years after the temperature reached at least 29°?
   A. 2,295   B. 1,717   C. 2,210   D. 4,543

9. In 2007, the event saw 288 participants, while in 2008 that number dropped to 173. Which of the following reasons BEST explains the drop in participants?
   A. The event had not been going on that long and people didn't know about it.
   B. The lake water wasn't cold enough to have people jump in.
   C. The temperature was too cold for many people who would have normally participated.
   D. None of the above reasons explain the drop in participants.

10. In the following list of numbers, how many times does 4 come just after 2 when 2 comes just after an odd number?
    2365247653898632488572486392424
    A. 2   B. 3   C. 4   D. 5

11. Which choice below lists the letter that is as far after B as S is after N in the alphabet?
    A. G   B. H   C. I   D. J

Questions 12-15.

DIRECTIONS: Questions 12 through 15 are to be answered on the basis of the following directory and list of changes.

Directory		
Name	Emp. Type	Position
Julie Taylor	Warehouse	Packer
James King	Office	Administrative Assistant
John Williams	Office	Salesperson
Ray Moore	Warehouse	Maintenance
Kathleen Byrne	Warehouse	Supervisor
Amy Jones	Office	Salesperson
Paul Jonas	Office	Salesperson
Lisa Wong	Warehouse	Loader
Eugene Lee	Office	Accountant
Bruce Lavine	Office	Manager
Adam Gates	Warehouse	Packer
Will Suter	Warehouse	Packer
Gary Lorper	Office	Accountant
Jon Adams	Office	Salesperson
Susannah Harper	Office	Salesperson

Directory Updates:
- Employee e-mail addresses will adhere to the following guidelines: lastnamefirstname@apexindustries.com (ex. Susannah Harper is harpersusannah@apexindustries.com). Currently, employees in the warehouse share one e-mail, distribution@apexindustries.com.
- The "Loader" position will now be referred to as "Specialist I"
- Adam Gates has accepted a Supervisor position within the Warehouse and is no longer a Packer. All warehouse employees report to the two Supervisors and all office employees report to the Manager.

12. Amy Jones tried to send an e-mail to Adam Gates, but it wouldn't send. Which of the following offers the BEST explanation? 12.____
    A. Amy put Adam's first name first and then his last name.
    B. Adam doesn't check his e-mail, so he wouldn't know if he received the e-mail or not.
    C. Adam does not have his own e-mail.
    D. Office employees are not allowed to send e-mails to each other.

13. How many Packers currently work for Apex Industries? 13.____
    A. 2   B. 3   C. 4   D. 5

14. What position does Lisa Wong currently hold? 14.____
    A. Specialist I   B. Secretary
    C. Administrative Assistant   D. Loader

15. If an employee wanted to contact the office manager, which of the following e-mails should the e-mail be sent to?
    A. officemanager@apexindustries.com
    B. brucelavine@apexindustries.com
    C. lavinebruce@apexindustries.com
    D. distribution@apexindustries.com

15.____

Questions 16-19.

DIRECTIONS: In answering Questions 16 through 19, compare the three names, numbers or addresses.

16. Smiley Yarnell   Smiley Yarnel   Smily Yarnell   16.____
    A. All three are exactly alike.
    B. The first and second are exactly alike.
    C. The second and third are exactly alike.
    D. All three are different.

17. 1583 Theater Drive   1583 Theater Drive   1583 Theatre Drive   17.____
    A. All three are exactly alike.
    B. The first and second are exactly alike.
    C. The second and third are exactly alike.
    D. All three are different.

18. 3341893212   3341893212   3341893212   18.____
    A. All three are exactly alike.
    B. The first and second are exactly alike.
    C. The second and third are exactly alike.
    D. All three are different.

19. Douglass Watkins   Douglas Watkins   Douglass Watkins   19.____
    A. All three are exactly alike.
    B. The first and third are exactly alike.
    C. The second and third are exactly alike.
    D. All three are different.

Questions 20-24.

DIRECTIONS: In answering Questions 20 through 24, you will be presented with a word. Choose the synonym that BEST represents the word in question.

20. Flexible   20.____
    A. delicate   B. inflammable   C. strong   D. pliable

21. Alternative   21.____
    A. choice   B. moderate   C. lazy   D. value

22. Corroborate
    A. examine   B. explain   C. verify   D. explain

23. Respiration
    A. recovery   B. breathing   C. sweating   D. selfish

24. Negligent
    A. lazy   B. moderate   C. hopeless   D. lax

25. Plumber is to Wrench as Painter is to
    A. pipe   B. shop   C. hammer   D. brush

KEY (CORRECT ANSWERS)

1.	D		11.	A
2.	A		12.	C
3.	D		13.	A
4.	C		14.	A
5.	B		15.	C
6.	C		16.	D
7.	C		17.	B
8.	B		18.	A
9.	C		19.	B
10.	C		20.	D

21. A
22. C
23. B
24. D
25. D

EXAMINATION SECTION
TEST 1

DIRECTIONS: Each question or incomplete statement is followed by several suggested answers or completions. Select the one that BEST answers the question or completes the statement. *PRINT THE LETTER OF THE CORRECT ANSWER IN THE SPACE AT THE RIGHT.*

Questions 1-5.

DIRECTIONS: Questions 1 through 5 consist of a sentence with an underlined word. For each question, select the choice that is CLOSEST in meaning to the underlined word.

EXAMPLE
This division reviews the fiscal reports of the agency.
In this sentence, the word *fiscal* means MOST NEARLY
    A. financial   B. critical   C. basic   D. personnel
The correct answer is A. "financial" because "financial" is closest to *fiscal*. Therefore, the answer is A.

1. Every good office worker needs basic skills.
   The word *basic* in this sentence means
       A. fundamental   B. advanced   C. unusual   D. outstanding

2. He turned out to be a good instructor.
   The word *instructor* in this sentence means
       A. student   B. worker   C. typist   D. teacher

3. The quantity of work in the office was under study.
   In this sentence, the word *quantity* means
       A. amount   B. flow   C. supervision   D. type

4. The morning was spent examining the time records.
   In this sentence, the word *examining* means
       A. distributing   B. collecting   C. checking   D. filing

5. The candidate filled in the proper spaces on the form.
   In this sentence, the word *proper* means
       A. blank   B. appropriate   C. many   D. remaining

Questions 6-8.

DIRECTIONS: Questions 6 through 8 are to be answered SOLELY on the basis of the information contained in the following paragraph.

The increase in the number of public documents in the last two centuries closely matches the increase in population in the United States. The great number of public documents has become a serious threat to their usefulness. It is necessary to have programs which will reduce the number of public documents that are kept and which will, at the same time, assure keeping those that have value. Such programs need a great deal of thought to have any success.

6. According to the above paragraph, public documents may be less useful if
   A. the files are open to the public
   B. the record room is too small
   C. the copying machine is operated only during normal working hours
   D. too many records are being kept

7. According to the above paragraph, the growth of the population in the United States has matched the growth in the quantity of public documents for a period of MOST NEARLY _____ years.
   A. 50   B. 100   C. 200   D. 300

8. According to the above paragraph, the increased number of public documents has made it necessary to
   A. find out which public documents are worth keeping
   B. reduce the great number of public documents by decreasing government services
   C. eliminate the copying of all original public documents
   D. avoid all new copying devices

Questions 9-10.

DIRECTIONS: Questions 9 and 10 are to be answered SOLELY on the basis of the information contained in the following paragraph.

The work goals of an agency can best be reached if the employees understand and agree with these goals. One way to gain such understanding and agreement is for management to encourage and seriously consider suggestions from employees in the setting of agency goals.

9. On the basis of the above paragraph, the BEST way to achieve the work goals of an agency is to
   A. make certain that employees work as hard as possible
   B. study the organizational structure of the agency
   C. encourage employees to think seriously about the agency's problems
   D. stimulate employee understanding of the work goals

10. On the basis of the above paragraph, understanding and agreement with agency 10.____
goals can be gained by
- A. allowing the employees to set agency goals
- B. reaching agency goals quickly
- C. legislative review of agency operations
- D. employee participation in setting agency goals

Questions 11-15.

DIRECTIONS: Each of Questions 11 through 15 consists of a group of four words. One word in each group is incorrectly spelled. For each question, print the letter of the correct answer in the space at the right that is the same as the letter next to the word which is INCORRECTLY spelled.

EXAMPLE

A. housing B. certain C. budgit D. money

The word "budgit" is incorrectly spelled, because the correct spelling should be "budget." Therefore, the correct answer is C.

11.	A. sentince	B. bulletin	C. notice	D. definition	11.____
12.	A. appointment	B. exactly	C. typest	D. light	12.____
13.	A. penalty	B. suparvise	C. consider	D. division	13.____
14.	A. schedule	B. accurate	C. corect	D. simple	14.____
15.	A. suggestion	B. installed	C. proper	D. agincy	15.____

Questions 16-20.

DIRECTIONS: Each Question 16 through 20 consists of a sentence which may be
- A. incorrect because of bad word usage, or
- B. incorrect because of bad punctuation, or
- C. incorrect because of bad spelling, or
- D. correct

Read each sentence carefully. Then print in the space at the right A, B, C, or D, according to the answer you choose from the four choices listed above. There is only one type of error in each incorrect sentence. If there is no error, the sentence is correct.

EXAMPLE

George Washington was the father of his contry.
This sentence is incorrect because of bad spelling ("contry" instead of "country").
Therefore, the answer is C.

16. The assignment was completed in record time but the payroll for it has not yet been preparid.

16.____

17. The operator, on the other hand, is willing to learn me how to use the mimeograph.

17.____

18. She is the prettiest of the three sisters.

18.____

19. She doesn't know; if the mail has arrived.

19.____

20. The doorknob of the office door is broke.

20.____

21. A clerk can process a form in 15 minutes.
    How many forms can that clerk process in six hours?
    A. 10   B. 21   C. 24   D. 90

21.____

22. An office staff consists of 120 people. Sixty of them have been assigned to a special project. Of the remaining staff, 20 answer the mail, 10 handle phone calls, and the rest operate the office machines.
    The number of people operating the office machines is
    A. 20   B. 30   C. 40   D. 45

22.____

23. An office worker received 65 applications but on the first day had to return 26 of them for being incomplete and on the second day 25 had to be returned for being incomplete.
    How many applications did NOT have to be returned?
    A. 10   B. 12   C. 14   D. 16

23.____

24. An office worker answered 63 phone calls in one day and 91 phone calls the next day.
    For these 2 days, what was the average number of phone calls he answered per day?
    A. 77   B. 28   C. 82   D. 93

24.____

25. An office worker processed 12 vouchers of $8.50 each, 3 vouchers of $3.68 each, and 2 vouchers of $1.29 each.
    The TOTAL dollar amount of these vouchers is
    A. $116.04   B. $117.52   C. $118.62   D. $119.04

25.____

KEY (CORRECT ANSWERS)

1.	A		11.	A
2.	D		12.	C
3.	A		13.	B
4.	C		14.	C
5.	B		15.	D
6.	D		16.	C
7.	C		17.	A
8.	A		18.	D
9.	D		19.	B
10.	D		20.	A

21. C
22. B
23. C
24. A
25. C

TEST 2

DIRECTIONS: Each question or incomplete statement is followed by several suggested answers or completions. Select the one that BEST answers the question or completes the statement. *PRINT THE LETTER OF THE CORRECT ANSWER IN THE SPACE AT THE RIGHT.*

Questions 1-5.

DIRECTIONS: Each Question from 1 through 5 lists four names. The names may not be exactly the same. Compare the names in each question and mark your answer
    A   if all the names are different
    B   if only two names are exactly the same
    C   if only three names are exactly the same
    D   if all four names are exactly the same
EXAMPLE
Jensen, Alfred E.
Jensen, Alfred E.
Jensan, Alfred E.
Jensen, Fred E.

Since the name Jensen, Alfred E. appears twice and is exactly the same in both places, the correct answer is B.

1.   A. Riviera, Pedro S.   B. Rivers, Pedro S.   1.____
     C. Riviera, Pedro N.   D. Riviera, Juan S.

2.   A. Guider, Albert   B. Guidar, Albert   2.____
     C. Giuder, Alfred   D. Guider, Albert

3.   A. Blum, Rona   B. Blum, Rona   3.____
     C. Blum, Rona   D. Blum, Rona

4.   A. Raugh, John   B. Raugh, James   4.____
     C. Raughe, John   D. Raugh, John

5.   A. Katz, Stanley   B. Katz, Stanley   5.____
     C. Katze, Stanley   D. Katz, Stanley

Questions 6-10.

DIRECTIONS: Each Question 6 through 10 consists of numbers or letters in Columns I and II. For each question, compare each line of Column I with its corresponding line in Column II and decide how many lines in Column I are EXACTLY the same as their corresponding lines in Column II. In your answer space, mark your answer
    A   if only ONE line in Column I is exactly the same as its corresponding line in Column II
    B   if only TWO lines in Column I are exactly the same as their corresponding lines in Column II

2 (#2)

    C if only THREE lines in Column I are exactly the same as their corresponding lines in Column II
    D if all FOUR lines in Column I are exactly the same as their corresponding lines in Column II

EXAMPLE

Column I	Column II
1776	1776
1865	1865
1945	1945
1976	1978

Only three lines in Column I are exactly the same as their corresponding lines in Column II. Therefore, the correct answer is C.

	Column I	Column II	
6.	5653 8727 ZPSS 4952	5653 8728 ZPSS 9453	6.____
7.	PNJP NJPJ JNPN PNJP	PNPJ NJPJ JNPN PNPJ	7.____
8.	effe uWvw KpGj vmnv	eFfe uWvw KpGg vmnv	8.____
9.	5232 PfrC zssz rwwr	5232 PfrN zzss rwww	9.____
10.	czws cecc thrm lwtz	czws cece thrm lwtz	10.____

Questions 11-15.

DIRECTIONS: Questions 11 through 15 have lines of letters and numbers. Each letter should be matched with its number in accordance with the following table.

Letter	F	R	C	A	W	L	E	N	B	T
Matching Number	0	1	2	3	4	5	6	7	8	9

From the table you can determine that the letter F has the matching number 0 below it, the letter R has the matching number 1 below, etc.

For each question, compare each line of letters and numbers carefully to see if each letter has its correct matching number. If all the letters and numbers are matched correctly in

none of the lines of the question, mark your answer A
only *one* of the lines of the question, mark your answer B
only *two* of the lines of the question, mark your answer C
all three lines of the question, mark your answer D

EXAMPLE

WBCR	4826
TLBF	9580
ATNE	3986

There is a mistake in the first line because the letter R should have its matching number 1 instead of the number 6.

The second line is correct because each letter shown has the correct matching number.

There is a mistake in the third line because the letter N should have the matching number 7 instead of the number 8.

Since all the letters and numbers are correct matched in only one of the lines in the sample, the correct answer is B.

11.
    EBCT 6829
    ATWR 3961
    NLBW 7584
    11.____

12.
    RNCT 1729
    LNCR 5728
    WAEB 5368
    12.____

13.
    NTWB 7948
    RABL 1385
    TAEF 9360
    13.____

14.
    LWRB 5417
    RLWN 1647
    CBWA 2843
    14.____

15.
    ABTC 3792
    WCER 5261
    AWCN 3417
    15.____

16. Your job often brings you into contact with the public.
    Of the following, it would be MOST desirable to explain the reasons for official actions to people coming into your office for assistance because such explanations
    A. help build greater understanding between the public and your agency
    B. help build greater self-confidence in city employees
    C. convince the public that nothing they do can upset a city employee
    D. show the public that city employees are intelligent
    16.____

17. Assume that you strongly dislike one of your co-workers.
    You should FIRST
    A. discuss your feeling with the co-worker
    B. demand a transfer to another office
    C. suggest to your supervisor that the co-worker should be observed carefully
    D. try to figure out the reason for this dislike before you say or do anything

18. An office worker who has problems accepting authority is MOST likely to find it difficult to
    A. obey rules
    B. understand people
    C. assist other employees
    D. follow complex instructions

19. The employees in your office have taken a dislike to one person and frequently annoy her.
    Your supervisor should
    A. transfer this person to another unit at the first opportunity
    B. try to find out the reason for the staff's attitude before doing anything about it
    C. threaten to transfer the first person observed bothering this person
    D. ignore the situation

20. Assume that your supervisor has asked a worker in your office to get a copy of a report out of the files. You notice the worker as accidentally pulled out the wrong report.
    Of the following, the BEST way for you to handle this situation is to tell
    A. the worker about all the difficulties that will result from this error
    B. the worker about her mistake in a nice way
    C. the worker to ignore this error
    D. your supervisor that this worker needs more training in how to use the files

21. Filing systems differ in their efficiency.
    Which of the following is the BEST way to evaluate the efficiency of a filing system? A
    A. number of times used per day
    B. amount of material that is received each day for filing
    C. amount of time it takes to locate material
    D. type of locking system used

22. In planning ahead so that a sufficient amount of general office supplies is always available, it would be LEAST important to find out the
    A. current office supply needs of the staff
    B. amount of office supplies used last year
    C. days and times that office supplies can be ordered
    D. agency goals and objectives

23. The MAIN reason for establishing routine office work procedures is that once a routine is established
    A. work need not be checked for accuracy
    B. all steps in the routine will take an equal amount of time to perform
    C. each time the job is repeated, it will take less time to perform
    D. each step in the routine will not have to be planned all over again each time

24. When an office machine centrally located in an agency must be shut down for repairs, the bureaus and divisions using this machine should be informed of the
    A. expected length of time before the machine will be in operation again
    B. estimated cost of repairs
    C. efforts being made to avoid future repairs
    D. type of new equipment which the agency may buy in the future to replace the machine being repaired

25. If the day's work is properly scheduled, the MOST important result would be that the
    A. supervisor will not have to do much supervision
    B. employee will know what to do next
    C. employee will show greater initiative
    D. job will become routine

KEY (CORRECT ANSWERS)

1.	A		11.	C
2.	B		12.	B
3.	D		13.	D
4.	B		14.	B
5.	C		15.	A
6.	B		16.	A
7.	B		17.	D
8.	B		18.	A
9.	A		19.	B
10.	C		20.	B

21.	C
22.	D
23.	D
24.	A
25.	B

EXAMINATION SECTION
TEST 1

DIRECTIONS: Each question or incomplete statement is followed by several suggested answers or completions. Select the one that BEST answers the question or completes the statement. *PRINT THE LETTER OF THE CORRECT ANSWER IN THE SPACE AT THE RIGHT.*

Questions 1-25.

DIRECTIONS: In each of Questions 1 through 25, select the lettered word or phrase which means MOST NEARLY the same as the capitalized word.

1. INTERROGATE
   A. question   B. arrest   C. search   D. rebuff

2. PERVERSE
   A. manageable   B. poetic
   C. contrary   D. patient

3. ADVOCATE
   A. champion   B. employ
   C. select   D. advise

4. APPARENT
   A. desirable   B. clear
   C. partial   D. possible

5. INSINUATE
   A. survey   B. strengthen
   C. suggest   D. insist

6. MOMENTOUS
   A. important   B. immediate   C. delayed   D. short

7. AUXILIARY
   A. exciting   B. assisting   C. upsetting   D. available

8. ADMONISH
   A. praise   B. increase   C. warn   D. polish

9. ANTICIPATE
   A. agree   B. expect   C. conceal   D. approve

10. APPREHEND
    A. confuse   B. sentence   C. release   D. seize

11. CLEMENCY
    A. silence   B. freedom   C. mercy   D. severity

12. THWART
    A. enrage   B. strike   C. choke   D. block

13. RELINQUISH
    A. stretch   B. give up   C. weaken   D. flee from
14. CURTAIL
    A. stop   B. reduce   C. repair   D. insult
15. INACCESSIBLE
    A. obstinate   B. unreachable
    C. unreasonable   D. puzzling
16. PERTINENT
    A. related   B. saucy   C. durable   D. impatient
17. INTIMIDATE
    A. encourage   B. hunt   C. beat   D. frighten
18. INTEGRITY
    A. honesty   B. wisdom
    C. understanding   D. persistence
19. UTILIZE
    A. use   B. manufacture
    C. help   D. include
20. SUPPLEMENT
    A. regulate   B. demand   C. add   D. answer
21. INDISPENSABLE
    A. essential   B. neglected
    C. truthful   D. unnecessary
22. ATTAIN
    A. introduce   B. spoil   C. achieve   D. study
23. PRECEDE
    A. break away   B. go ahead
    C. begin   D. come before
24. HAZARD
    A. penalty   B. adventure   C. handicap   D. danger
25. DETRIMENTAL
    A. uncertain   B. harmful   C. fierce   D. horrible

KEY (CORRECT ANSWERS)

1. A	6. A	11. C	16. A	21. A
2. C	7. B	12. D	17. D	22. C
3. A	8. C	13. B	18. A	23. D
4. B	9. B	14. B	19. A	24. D
5. C	10. D	15. B	20. C	25. B

TEST 2

DIRECTIONS: Each question or incomplete statement is followed by several suggested answers or completions. Select the one that BEST answers the question or completes the statement. *PRINT THE LETTER OF THE CORRECT ANSWER IN THE SPACE AT THE RIGHT.*

Questions 1-20.

DIRECTIONS: In each of Questions 1 through 20, select the lettered word or phrase which means MOST NEARLY the same as the capitalized word.

1. IMPLY
   - A. agree to
   - B. hint at
   - C. laugh at
   - D. mimic
   - E. reduce

2. APPRAISAL
   - A. allowance
   - B. composition
   - C. prohibition
   - D. quantity
   - E. valuation

3. DISBURSE
   - A. approve
   - B. expend
   - C. prevent
   - D. relay
   - E. restrict

4. POSTERITY
   - A. back payment
   - B. current procedure
   - C. final effort
   - D. future generations
   - E. rare specimen

5. PUNCTUAL
   - A. clear
   - B. honest
   - C. polite
   - D. prompt
   - E. prudent

6. PRECARIOUS
   - A. abundant
   - B. alarmed
   - C. cautious
   - D. insecure
   - E. placid

7. FOSTER
   - A. delegate
   - B. demote
   - C. encourage
   - D. plead
   - E. surround

8. PINNACLE
   - A. center
   - B. crisis
   - C. outcome
   - D. peak
   - E. personification

9. COMPONENT
   - A. flattery
   - B. opposite
   - C. part
   - D. revision
   - E. trend

10. SOLICIT
    - A. ask
    - B. prohibit
    - C. promise
    - D. revoke
    - E. surprise

1. ___
2. ___
3. ___
4. ___
5. ___
6. ___
7. ___
8. ___
9. ___
10. ___

11. LIAISON
    - A. asset
    - B. coordination
    - C. difference
    - D. policy
    - E. procedure

12. ALLEGE
    - A. assert
    - B. break
    - C. irritate
    - D. reduce
    - E. wait

13. INFILTRATION
    - A. consumption
    - B. disposal
    - C. enforcement
    - D. penetration
    - E. seizure

14. SALVAGE
    - A. announce
    - B. combine
    - C. prolong
    - D. save
    - E. try

15. MOTIVE
    - A. attack
    - B. favor
    - C. incentive
    - D. patience
    - E. tribute

16. PROVOKE
    - A. adjust
    - B. incite
    - C. leave
    - D. obtain
    - E. practice

17. SURGE
    - A. branch
    - B. contract
    - C. revenge
    - D. rush
    - E. want

18. MAGNIFY
    - A. attract
    - B. demand
    - C. generate
    - D. increase
    - E. puzzle

19. PREPONDERANCE
    - A. decision
    - B. judgment
    - C. outweighing
    - D. submission
    - E. warning

20. ABATE
    - A. assist
    - B. coerce
    - C. diminish
    - D. indulge
    - E. trade

Questions 21-30.

DIRECTIONS: In each of Questions 21 through 30, select the lettered word or phrase which means MOST NEARLY, the same as, or the opposite of, the capitalized word.

21. VINDICTIVE
    - A. centrifugal
    - B. forgiving
    - C. molten
    - D. tedious
    - E. vivacious

22. SCOPE
    - A. compact
    - B. detriment
    - C. facsimile
    - D. potable
    - E. range

23. HINDER
    A. amplify   B. aver   C. method
    D. observe   E. retard
    23.___

24. IRATE
    A. adhere   B. angry   C. authentic
    D. peremptory   E. vacillate
    24.___

25. APATHY
    A. accessory   B. availability   C. fervor
    D. pacify   E. stride
    25.___

26. LUCRATIVE
    A. effective   B. imperfect   C. injurious
    D. timely   E. worthless
    26.___

27. DIVERSITY
    A. convection   B. slip   C. temerity
    D. uniformity   E. viscosity
    27.___

28. OVERT
    A. laugh   B. lighter   C. orifice
    D. quay   E. sly
    28.___

29. SPORADIC
    A. divide   B. incumbrance   C. livid
    D. occasional   E. original
    29.___

30. PREVARICATE
    A. hesitate   B. increase   C. lie
    D. procrastinate   E. reject
    30.___

KEY (CORRECT ANSWERS)

1.	B	11.	B	21.	B
2.	E	12.	A	22.	E
3.	B	13.	D	23.	E
4.	D	14.	D	24.	B
5.	D	15.	C	25.	C
6.	D	16.	B	26.	E
7.	C	17.	D	27.	D
8.	D	18.	D	28.	E
9.	C	19.	C	29.	D
10.	A	20.	C	30.	C

TEST 3

DIRECTIONS: Each question or incomplete statement is followed by several suggested answers or completions. Select the one that BEST answers the question or completes the statement. *PRINT THE LETTER OF THE CORRECT ANSWER IN THE SPACE AT THE RIGHT.*

Questions 1-30.

DIRECTIONS: In each of Questions 1 through 30, select the lettered word which means MOST NEARLY the same as the capitalized word.

1. AVARICE
   A. flight B. greed C. pride D. thrift

2. PREDATORY
   A. offensive B. plundering
   C. previous D. timeless

3. VINDICATE
   A. clear B. conquer C. correct D. illustrate

4. INVETERATE
   A. backward B. erect C. habitual D. lucky

5. DISCERN
   A. describe B. fabricate C. recognize D. seek

6. COMPLACENT
   A. indulgent B. listless C. overjoyed D. satisfied

7. ILLICIT
   A. insecure B. unclear C. unlawful D. unlimited

8. PROCRASTINATE
   A. declare B. multiply C. postpone D. steal

9. IMPASSIVE
   A. calm B. frustrated
   C. thoughtful D. unhappy

10. AMICABLE
    A. cheerful B. flexible
    C. friendly D. poised

11. FEASIBLE
    A. breakable B. easy
    C. likeable D. practicable

12. INNOCUOUS
    A. harmless B. insecure
    C. insincere D. unfavorable

13. OSTENSIBLE
    A. apparent   B. hesitant   C. reluctant   D. showy
    13.___

14. INDOMITABLE
    A. excessive   B. unconquerable
    C. unreasonable   D. unthinkable
    14.___

15. CRAVEN
    A. cowardly   B. hidden   C. miserly   D. needed
    15.___

16. ALLAY
    A. discuss   B. quiet   C. refine   D. remove
    16.___

17. ALLUDE
    A. denounce   B. refer   C. state   D. support
    17.___

18. NEGLIGENCE
    A. carelessness   B. denial
    C. objection   D. refusal
    18.___

19. AMEND
    A. correct   B. destroy   C. end   D. list
    19.___

20. RELEVANT
    A. conclusive   B. careful
    C. obvious   D. related
    20.___

21. VERIFY
    A. challenge   B. change   C. confirm   D. reveal
    21.___

22. INSIGNIFICANT
    A. incorrect   B. limited
    C. unimportant   D. undesirable
    22.___

23. RESCIND
    A. annul   B. deride   C. extol   D. indulge
    23.___

24. AUGMENT
    A. alter   B. increase   C. obey   D. perceive
    24.___

25. AUTONOMOUS
    A. conceptual   B. constant
    C. defamatory   D. independent
    25.___

26. TRANSCRIPT
    A. copy   B. report   C. sentence   D. termination
    26.___

27. DISCORDANT
    A. quarrelsome   B. comprised
    C. effusive   D. harmonious
    27.___

28. DISTEND
    A. constrict   B. dilate   C. redeem   D. silence
    28.___

29. EMANATE
    A. bridge   B. coherency   C. conquer   D. flow

30. EXULTANT
    A. easily upset
    B. in high spirits
    C. subject to moods
    D. very much over-priced

KEY (CORRECT ANSWERS)

1. B	11. D	21. C
2. B	12. A	22. C
3. A	13. A	23. A
4. C	14. B	24. B
5. C	15. A	25. D
6. D	16. B	26. A
7. C	17. B	27. A
8. C	18. A	28. B
9. A	19. A	29. D
10. C	20. D	30. B

EXAMINATION SECTION
TEST 1

DIRECTIONS: Each question or incomplete statement is followed by several suggested answers or completions. Select the one that BEST answers the question or completes the statement. *PRINT THE LETTER OF THE CORRECT ANSWER IN THE SPACE AT THE RIGHT.*

Questions 1-25

Each sentence in questions 1-25 includes four words with letters over them. One of these words has been typed incorrectly. Indicate the misspelled word by printing the letter in the space at the right.

1.
        A   B
If the administrator attempts to withold information,
       C
there is a good likelihood that there will be serious
  D
repercussions.
                                            1.____

2.
    A   B   C
He condescended to apologize, but we felt that a beligerent
              D
person should not occupy an influential position.
                                            2.____

3.
           A   B   C
Despite the sporadic delinquent payments of his indebted-
            D
ness, Mr. Johnson has been an exemplery customer.
                                            3.____

4.
        A   B
He was appreciative of the support he consistantly
  C   D
acquired, but he felt that he had waited an inordinate length of time for it.
                                            4.____

5.
     A   B
Undeniably they benefited from the establishment of a
  C   D
receivership, but the question or statutary limitations remained unresolved.
                                            5.____

6.
         A
Mr. Smith profered his hand as an indication that he
        B   C
considered it a viable contract, but Mr. Nelson alluded
            D
to the fact that his colleagues had not been consulted.

6.____

7.
                    A   B
The treatments were beneficial according to the optomo-
             C   D
trists, and the consensus was that minimal improvement
could be expected.

7.____

8.
    A
Her frivalous manner was unbecoming because the air of
   B   C   D
solemnity at the cemetery was pervasive.

8.____

9.
       A
The clandestine meetings were designed to make the two
 B   C
adversaries more amicible, but they served only to
        D
intensify their emnity.

9.____

10.
              A
Do you think that his innovative ideas and financial
 B   C   D
acumen will help stabalize the fluctuations of the stock
market?

10.____

11.
          A
In order to keep a perpetual inventory, you will have to
    B   C   D
keep an uninterrupted surveillance of all the miscellaneous
stock.

11.____

12.
       A
She used the art of pursuasion on the children because
      B   C   D
she found that caustic remarks had no perceptible effect
on their behavior.

12.____

13.

     A   B
His sacreligious outbursts offended his constituents, and
       C   D
he was summarily removed from office by the City Council.

14.

    A   B
They exhorted the contestants to greater efforts, but the
 C
exhorbitant costs in terms of energy expended resulted in
       D
a feeling of lethargy.

15.

       A   B
Since he was knowledgable about illicit drugs, he was
   C   D
served with a subpoena to appear for the prosecution.

16.

      A   B
In spite of his lucid statements, they denigrated his
            C   D
report and decided it should be succintly paraphrased.

17.

           A   B
The discussion was not germane to the contraversy, but
 C   D
the indicted man's insistence on further talk was allowed.

18.

    A   B
The legislators were enervated by the distances they had
 C   D
traveled during the election year to fulfil their speaking
engagements.

19.

    A   B   C
The plaintiffs' attorneys charged the defendant in the
  D
case with felonious assault.

20.
          A   B
It is symptomatic of the times that we try to placate
                                C
all, but a proposal for new forms of disciplinery action
            D
was promulgated by the staff.

21.
  A
A worrysome situation has developed as a result of the
      B   C
assessment that absenteeism is increasing despite our
      D
conscientious efforts.

22.
    A   B
I concurred with the credit manager that it was practi-
                      C
cable to charge purchases on a biennial basis, and the
                 D
company agreed to adhear to this policy.

23.
           A   B   C
The pastor was chagrined and embarassed by the irreverent
        D
conduct of one of his parishioners.

24.
    A   B   C
His inate seriousness was belied by his flippant
D
demeanor.

25.
     A   B   C
It was exceedingly regrettable that the excessive number
  D
of challanges in the court delayed the start of the
trial.

Questions 26-45.

In each of the following sentences, numbered 26-45, there may be an error. Indicate the appropriate correction by printing the corresponding letter in the space at the right. If the sentence is correct as is, indicate this by printing the corresponding letter in the space at the right. Unnecessary changes will be considered incorrect.

26. In that building there seemed to be representatives of Teachers College, the Veterans Bureau, and the Businessmen's Association.   26.____

    A. Teacher's College
    B. Veteran's Bureau
    C. Businessmens Association
    D. correct as is

27. In his travels, he visited St. Paul, San Francisco, Springfield, Ohio, and Washington, D.C..   27.____

    A. Ohio and
    B. Saint Paul
    C. Washington, D.C.
    D. correct as is

28. As a result of their purchasing a controlling interest in the syndicate, it was well-known that the Bureau of Labor Statistics' calculations would be unimportant.   28.____

    A. of them purchasing
    B. well known
    C. Statistics
    D. correct as is

29. Walter Scott, Jr.'s, attempt to emulate his father's success was doomed to failure.   29.____

    A. Junior's,
    B. Scott's, Jr.,
    C. Scott, Jr.'s attempt
    D. correct as is

30. About B.C. 250 the Romans invaded Great Britain, and remains of their highly developed civilization can still be seen.   30.____

    A. 250 B.C.
    B. Britain and
    C. highly-developed
    D. correct as is

31. The two boss's sons visited the children's department.   31.____

    A. bosses
    B. bosses'
    C. childrens'
    D. correct as is

32. Miss Amex not only approved the report, but also decided that it needed no revision.   32.____

    A. report; but
    B. report but
    C. report. But
    D. correct as is

33. Here's brain food in a jiffy--economical too!   33.____

    A. economical too!
    B. 'brain food'
    C. jiffy-economical
    D. correct as is

34. She said, "He likes the "Gatsby Look" very much."   34.____

    A. said "He
    B. "he
    C. 'Gatsby Look'
    D. correct as is

35. We anticipate that we will be able to visit them briefly in Los Angeles on Wednesday after a 5-day visit.

    A. Wednes-
    B. 5-day
    C. briefly
    D. correct as is

36. She passed all her tests, and, she now has a good position.

    A. tests, and she
    B. past
    C. tests;
    D. correct as is

37. The billing clerk said, "I will send the bill today"; however, that was a week ago, and it hasn't arrived yet!

    A. today;"
    B. today,"
    C. ago and
    D. correct as is

38. "She types at more-than-average speed," Miss Smith said, "but I feel that it is a result of marvelous concentration and self control on her part."

    A. more than average
    B. "But
    C. self-control
    D. correct as is

39. The state of Alaska, the largest state in the union, is also the northernmost state.

    A. Union
    B. Northernmost State
    C. State of Alaska
    D. correct as is

40. The memoirs of Ex-President Nixon, will sell more copies than Six Crises, the book he wrote in the 60's.

    A. Six Crises
    B. ex-President
    C. 60s
    D. correct as is

41. He spoke on his favorite topic, "Why We Will Win." (How could I stop him?)

    A. Win".
    B. him?).
    C. him)?
    D. correct as is

42. "All any insurance policy is, is a contract for services," said my insurance agent, Mr. Newton.

    A. Insurance Policy
    B. Insurance Agent
    C. policy is is a
    D. correct as is

43. Inasmuch as the price list has not been up dated, we should send it to the printer.

    A. In as much
    B. updated
    C. pricelist
    D. correct as is

44. We feel that "Our know-how" is responsible for the improvement in technical developments.

    A. "our
    B. know how
    C. that,
    D. correct as is

45. Did Cortez conquer the Incas? the Aztecs? the South American Indians?

    A. Incas, the Aztecs, the South American Indians?
    B. Incas; the Aztecs; the South American Indians?
    C. south American Indians?
    D. correct as is

Questions 46-70.

In the article which follows, certain words or groups of words are underlined and numbered. The underlined word or group of words may be incorrect because they present an error in grammer, usage, sentence structure, capitalization, diction, or punctuation. For each numbered word or group of words, there is an identically numbered question consisting of four choices based only on the underlined portion. For each question numbered 46-70, indicate the best choice by printing the corresponding letter in the space at the right. <u>Unnecessary changes will be considered incorrect.</u>

TIGERS VIE FOR CITY CHAMPIONSHIP

In their second year of varsity football, the North Side Tigers have gained a shot at the city championship. Last Saturday in the play-offs, the Tigers defeated the Western High School
<u>46</u>
Cowboys, <u>thus eliminated that team</u> from contention. Most of the credit for the team's improvement must go to Joe Harris, the
   <u>47</u>
coach. <u>To play as well as they do</u> now, the coach must have given the team superior instruction. There is no doubt that, <u>if a
   48
coach is effective, his influence is over</u> many young minds.

With this major victory behind them, the Tigers can now look
   <u>49</u>
forward <u>to meet</u> the defending champions, the Revere Minutemen, in the finals.
   <u>50</u>

The win over the Cowboys was <u>due to</u> North Side's supremacy in the air. The Tigers' players have the advantage of strength
   <u>51</u>
and of <u>being speedy</u>. Our sterling quarterback, Butch Carter, a
   <u>52</u>
master of the long pass, used <u>these kind of passes</u> to bedevil the
   <u>53</u>
boys from Western. As a matter of fact, if the Tigers <u>would have used</u> the passing offense earlier in the game, the score would have been more one sided. Butch, by the way, our all-around senior student, has already been tapped for bigger things. Having the
   <u>54</u>
highest marks in his class, <u>Barton College has offered him a scholarship</u>.

The team's defense is another story. During the last few
   <u>55</u>
weeks, neither the linebackers nor the safety man <u>have shown</u> sufficient ability to contain their opponents' running game. In
   <u>56</u>
the city final, <u>the defensive unit's failing to complete it's assignments</u> may lead to disaster. However, the coach said that
   <u>57</u>
this unit <u>not only has been cooperative, but also the coach</u> praised their eagerness to learn. He also said that this team
   <u>58</u>

has not and never will give up. This kind of spirit is contag-
            59
ious, therefore I predict that the Tigers will win because I have
     60
affection and full confidence in the team.
    One of the happy surprises this season is Peter Yisko, our
                  61
punter. Peter is in the United States for only two years. When
he was in grammar school in the old country, it was not necessary
                62
for him to have studied hard. Now, he depends on the football
                                                 63
team to help him with his English. Everybody but the team mascot
and I have been pressed into service. Peter was ineligible last
                        64
year when he learned that he would only obtain half of the credits
he had completed in Europe. Nevertheless, he attended occasional
practice sessions, but he soon found out that, if one wants to be
                    65
a successful player, you must realize that regular practice is
required. In fact, if a team is to be successful, it is necessary
            66
that everyone be present for all practice sessions. "The life of
               67
a football player," says Peter, "is better than a scholar."
Facing the Minutemen, the Tigers will meet their most
                                  68
formidable opposition yet. This team is not only gaining a bad
reputation but also indulging in illegal practices on the field.
            69
They can't hardly object to us being technical about penalties
under these circumstances. As far as the Minutemen are concerned,
            70
a victory will taste sweet like a victory should.

46. A. , that eliminated that team   46.___
     B. and they were eliminated
     C. and eliminated them
     D. correct as is

47. A. To make them play as well as they do   47.___
     B. Having played so well
     C. After they played so well
     D. correct as is

48. A. if coaches are effective; they have influence over   48.___
     B. to be effective, a coach influences
     C. if a coach is effective, he influences
     D. correct as is

49.
- A. to meet with
- B. to meeting
- C. to a meeting of
- D. correct as is

50.
- A. because of
- B. on account *of*
- C. motivated by
- D. correct as is

51.
- A. operating swiftly
- B. speed
- C. running speedily
- D. correct as is

52.
- A. these kinds of pass
- B. this kind of passes
- C. this kind of pass
- D. correct as is

53.
- A. would be used
- B. had used
- C. were using
- D. correct as is

54.
- A. he was offered a scholarship by Barton College.
- B. Barton College offered a scholarship to him.
- C. a scholarship was offered him by Barton College.
- D. correct as is

55.
- A. had shown
- B. were showing
- C. has shown
- D. correct as is

56.
- A. the defensive unit failing to complete its assignment
- B. the defensive unit's failing to complete its assignment
- C. the defensive unit failing to complete it's assignment
- D. correct as is

57.
- A. has been not only cooperative, but also eager to learn
- B. has not only been cooperative, but also shows eagerness to learn
- C. has been not only cooperative, but also they were eager to learn
- D. correct as is

58.
- A. has not given up and never will
- B. has not and never would give up
- C. has not given up and never will give up
- D. correct as is

59.
- A. .Therefore
- B. : therefore
- C. --therefore
- D. correct as is

60.
  A. full confidence and affection for
  B. affection for and full confidence in
  C. affection and full confidence concerning
  D. correct as is

61.
  A. is living   B. was living
  C. has been   D. correct as is

62.
  A. to study   B. to be studying
  C. to have been studying   D. correct as is

63.
  A. but the team mascot and me has
  B. but the team mascot and myself has
  C. but the team mascot and me have
  D. correct as is

64.
  A. only learned that he would obtain half
  B. learned that he would obtain only half
  C. learned that he only would obtain half
  D. correct as is

65.
  A. a person   B. everyone
  C. one   D. correct as is

66.
  A. is   B. will be
  C. shall be   D. correct as is

67.
  A. to be a scholar   B. being a scholar
  C. that of a scholar   D. correct as is

68.
  A. not only is gaining a bad reputation
  B. is gaining not only a bad reputation
  C. is not gaining only a bad reputation
  D. correct as is

69.
  A. can hardly object to us being
  B. can hardly object to our being
  C. can't hardly object to our being
  D. correct as is

70.
  A. victory will taste sweet like it should.
  B. victory will taste sweetly as it should taste.
  C. victory will taste sweet as a victory should.
  D. correct as is

KEY (CORRECT ANSWERS

1. B	16. C	31. B	46. C	61. C
2. C	17. B	32. B	47. A	62. A
3. D	18. D	33. D	48. C	63. A
4. B	19. B	34. C	49. B	64. B
5. D	20. C	35. B	50. A	65. C
6. A	21. A	36. A	51. B	66. D
7. B	22. D	37. D	52. C	67. C
8. A	23. B	38. D	53. B	68. D
9. C	24. A	39. A	54. D	69. A
10. C	25. D	40. B	55. C	70. C
11. D	26. D	41. D	56. B	
12. A	27. C	42. D	57. A	
13. A	28. B	43. B	58. B	
14. C	29. D	44. A	59. A	
15. A	30. A	45. D	60. B	

SPELLING

EXAMINATION SECTION

TEST 1

DIRECTIONS: Each question or incomplete statement is followed by several suggested answers or completions. Select the one that BEST answers the question or completes the statement. *PRINT THE LETTER OF THE CORRECT ANSWER IN THE SPACE AT THE RIGHT.*

Questions 1-5.

DIRECTIONS: Questions 1 through 5 consist of four words. Indicate the letter of the word that is CORRECTLY spelled.

1. A. harassment B. harrasment 1._____
 C. harasment D. harrassment

2. A. maintainance B. maintenence 2._____
 C. maintainence D. maintenance

3. A. comparable B. comprable 3._____
 C. comparible D. commparable

4. A. suficient B. sufficiant 4._____
 C. sufficient D. suficiant

5. A. fairly B. fairley C. farely D. fairlie 5._____

Questions 6-10.

DIRECTIONS: Questions 6 through 10 consist of four words. Indicate the letter of the word that is INCORRECTLY spelled.

6. A. pallor B. ballid C. ballet D. pallid 6._____

7. A. urbane B. surburbane 7._____
 C. interurban D. urban

8. A. facial B. physical C. fiscle D. muscle 8._____

9. A. interceed B. benefited 9._____
 C. analogous D. altogether

10. A. seizure B. irrelevant 10._____
 C. inordinate D. dissapproved

97

KEY (CORRECT ANSWERS)

1. A
2. D
3. A
4. C
5. A
6. B
7. B
8. C
9. A
10. D

TEST 2

DIRECTIONS: Each of Questions 1 through 15 consists of two words preceded by the letters A and B. In each question, one of the words may be spelled INCORRECTLY or both words may be spelled CORRECTLY. If one of the words in a question is spelled INCORRECTLY, print in the space at the right the capital letter preceding the INCORRECTLY spelled word. If both words are spelled CORRECTLY, print the letter C.

1. A. easely   B. readily   1.____
2. A. pursue   B. decend   2.____
3. A. measure   B. laboratory   3.____
4. A. exausted   B. traffic   4.____
5. A. discussion   B. unpleasant   5.____
6. A. campaign   B. murmer   6.____
7. A. guarantee   B. sanatary   7.____
8. A. communication   B. safty   8.____
9. A. numerus   B. celebration   9.____
10. A. nourish   B. begining   10.____
11. A. courious   B. witness   11.____
12. A. undoubtedly   B. thoroughly   12.____
13. A. accessible   B. artifical   13.____
14. A. feild   B. arranged   14.____
15. A. admittence   B. hastily   15.____

KEY (CORRECT ANSWERS)

1. A   6. B   11. A
2. B   7. B   12. C
3. C   8. B   13. B
4. A   9. A   14. A
5. C   10. B   15. A

TEST 3

DIRECTIONS: In each of the following sentences, one word is misspelled. Following each sentence is a list of four words taken from the sentence. Indicate the letter of the word which is MISSPELLED in the sentence. *PRINT THE LETTER OF THE CORRECT ANSWER IN THE SPACE AT THE RIGHT.*

1. The placing of any inflammable substance in any building, or the placing of any device or contrivance capable of producing fire, for the purpose of causing a fire is an attempt to burn.
   A. inflammable
   B. substance
   C. device
   D. contrivence

   1._____

2. The word *break* also means obtaining an entrance into a building by any artifice used for that purpose, or by collussion with any person therein.
   A. obtaining
   B. entrance
   C. artifice
   D. colussion

   2._____

3. Any person who with intent to provoke a breech of the peace causes a disturbance or is offensive to others may be deemed to have committed disorderly conduct.
   A. breech
   B. disturbance
   C. offensive
   D. committed

   3._____

4. When the offender inflicts a grevious harm upon the person from whose possession, or in whose presence, property is taken, he is guilty of robbery.
   A. offender
   B. grevious
   C. possession
   D. presence

   4._____

5. A person who wilfuly encourages or advises another person in attempting to take the latter's life is guilty of a felony.
   A. wilfuly
   B. encourages
   C. advises
   D. attempting

   5._____

6. He maliciously demurred to an ajournment of the proceedings.
   A. maliciously
   B. demurred
   C. ajournment
   D. proceedings

   6._____

7. His innocence at that time is irrelevant in view of his more recent villianous demeanor.
   A. innocence
   B. irrelevant
   C. villianous
   D. demeanor

   7._____

8. The mischievous boys aggrevated the annoyance of their neighbor.
   A. mischievous
   B. aggrevated
   C. annoyance
   D. neighbor

   8._____

2 (#3)

9. While his perseverence was commendable, his judgment was debatable. 9.____
   A. perseverence   B. commendable
   C. judgment   D. debatable

10. He was hoping the appeal would facilitate his aquittal. 10.____
    A. hoping   B. appeal
    C. facilitate   D. aquittal

11. It would be preferable for them to persue separate courses. 11.____
    A. preferable   B. persue
    C. separate   D. courses

12. The litigant was complimented on his persistance and achievement. 12.____
    A. litigant   B. complimented
    C. persistance   D. achievement

13. Ocassionally there are discrepancies in the descriptions of miscellaneous items. 13.____
    A. ocassionally   B. discrepancies
    C. descriptions   D. miscellaneous

14. The councilmanic seargent-at-arms enforced the prohibition. 14.____
    A. councilmanic   B. seargeant-at-arms
    C. enforced   D. prohibition

15. The teacher had an ingenious device for maintaining attendance. 15.____
    A. ingenious   B. device
    C. maintaning   D. attendance

16. A worrysome situation has developed as a result of the assessment that absenteeism is increasing despite our conscientious efforts. 16.____
    A. worrysome   B. assessment
    C. absenteeism   D. conscientious

17. I concurred with the credit manager that it was practicable to charge purchases on a biennial basis, and the company agreed to adhear to this policy. 17.____
    A. concurred   B. practicable
    C. biennial   D. adhear

18. The pastor was chagrined and embarassed by the irreverent conduct of one of his parishioners. 18.____
    A. chagrined   B. embarassed
    C. irreverent   D. parishioners

19. His inate seriousness was belied by his flippant demeanor. 19.____
    A. inate   B. belied
    C. flippant   D. demeanor

20. It was exceedingly regrettable that the excessive number of challenges in the court delayed the start of the trial.
    A. exceedingly
    B. regrettable
    C. excessive
    D. challanges

20.____

KEY (CORRECT ANSWERS)

1.	D	11.	B
2.	D	12.	C
3.	A	13.	A
4.	B	14.	B
5.	A	15.	C
6.	C	16.	A
7.	C	17.	D
8.	B	18.	B
9.	A	19.	A
10.	D	20.	D

TEST 4

Questions 1-11.

DIRECTIONS: Each question consists of three words in each question, one of the words may be spelled incorrectly or all three may be spelled correctly. For each question if one of the words is spelled INCORRECTLY, write the letter of the incorrect word in the space at the right. If all three words are spelled CORRECTLY, write the letter D in the space at the right.

SAMPLE I: (A) guide   (B) departmint   (C) stranger
SAMPLE II: (A) comply   (B) valuable   (C) window
In Sample I, departmint is incorrect. It should be spelled department.
Therefore, B is the answer.
In Sample II, all three words are spelled correctly. Therefore, D is the answer.

1.	A. argument	B. reciept	C. complain		1._____
2.	A. sufficient	B. postpone	C. visible		2._____
3.	A. expirience	B. dissatisly	C. alternate		3._____
4.	A. occurred	B. noticable	C. appendix		4._____
5.	A. anxious	B. guarantee	C. calendar		5._____
6.	A. sincerely	B. affectionately	C. truly		6._____
7.	A. excellant	B. verify	C. important		7._____
8.	A. error	B. quality	C. enviroment		8._____
9.	A. exercise	B. advance	C. pressure		9._____
10.	A. citizen	B. expence	C. memory		10._____
11.	A. flexable	B. focus	C. forward		11._____

Questions 12-15.

DIRECTIONS: Each of Questions 12 through 15 consists of a group of four words. Examine each group carefully; then in the space at the right, indicate
A. if only one word in the group is spelled correctly
B. if two words in the group are spelled correctly
C. if three words in the group are spelled correctly
D. if all four words in the group are spelled correctly

12. Wendsday, particular, similar, hunderd   12._____

103

13. realize, judgment, opportunities, consistent   13.____

14. equel, principle, assistense, committee   14.____

15. simultaneous, privilege, advise, ocassionaly   15.____

KEY (CORRECT ANSWERS)

1.	B	6.	D	11.	A
2.	D	7.	A	12.	B
3.	A	8.	C	13.	D
4.	B	9.	D	14.	A
5.	C	10.	B	15.	C

TEST 5

DIRECTIONS: Each of Questions 1 through 15 consists of two words preceded by the letters A and B. In each item, one of the words may be spelled INCORRECTLY or both words may be spelled CORRECTLY. If one of the words in a question is spelled INCORRECTLY, print in the space at the right the letter preceding the INCORRECTLY spelled word. If bot words are spelled CORRECTLY, print the letter C.

1. A. justified   B. offering   1._____
2. A. predjudice   B. license   2._____
3. A. label   B. pamphlet   3._____
4. A. bulletin   B. physical   4._____
5. A. assure   B. exceed   5._____
6. A. advantagous   B. evident   6._____
7. A. benefit   B. occured   7._____
8. A. acquire   B. graditude   8._____
9. A. amenable   B. boundry   9._____
10. A. deceive   B. voluntary   10._____
11. A. imunity   B. conciliate   11._____
12. A. acknoledge   B. presume   12._____
13. A. substitute   B. prespiration   13._____
14. A. reputable   B. announce   14._____
15. A. luncheon   B. wretched   15._____

KEY (CORRECT ANSWERS)

1.	C	6.	A	11.	A
2.	A	7.	B	12.	A
3.	C	8.	B	13.	B
4.	C	9.	B	14.	A
5.	C	10.	C	15.	C

TEST 6

DIRECTIONS: Questions 1 through 15 contain lists of words, one of which is misspelled. Indicate the MISSPELLED word in each group. *PRINT THE LETTER OF THE CORRECT ANSWER IN THE SPACE AT THE RIGHT.*

1. A. felony   B. lacerate   1._____
   C. cancellation   D. seperate

2. A. batallion   B. beneficial   2._____
   C. miscellaneous   D. secretary

3. A. camouflage   B. changeable   3._____
   C. embarrass   D. inoculate

4. A. beneficial   B. disasterous   4._____
   C. incredible   D. miniature

5. A. auxilliary   B. hypocrisy   5._____
   C. phlegm   D. vengeance

6. A. aisle   B. cemetary   6._____
   C. courtesy   D. extraordinary

7. A. crystallize   B. innoculate   7._____
   C. eminent   D. symmetrical

8. A. judgment   B. maintainance   8._____
   C. bouillon   D. eery

9. A. isosceles   B. ukulele   9._____
   C. mayonaise   D. iridescent

10. A. remembrance   B. occurence   10._____
    C. correspondence   D. countenance

11. A. corpuscles   B. mischievous   11._____
    C. batchelor   D. bulletin

12. A. terrace   B. banister   12._____
    C. concrete   D. masonery

13. A. balluster   B. gutter   13._____
    C. latch   D. bridging

14. A. personnell   B. navel   14._____
    C. therefor   D. emigrant

106

15. A. committee B. submiting
    C. amendment D. electorate   15._____

KEY (CORRECT ANSWERS)

1.	D	6.	B	11.	C
2.	A	7.	B	12.	D
3.	C	8.	B	13.	A
4.	B	9.	C	14.	A
5.	A	10.	B	15.	B

TEST 7

Questions 1-5.

DIRECTIONS: Questions 1 through 5 consist of groups of four words. Select answer
A if only one word is spelled correctly in a group
B if TWO words are spelled correctly in a group
C if THREE words are spelled correctly in a group
D if all FOUR words are spelled correctly in a group.

1. counterfeit, embarass, panicky, supercede 1.____

2. benefited, personnel, questionnaire, unparalelled 2.____

3. bankruptcy, describable, proceed, vacuum 3.____

4. handicapped, mispell, offerred, pilgrimmage 4.____

5. corduroy, interfere, privilege, separator 5.____

Questions 6-10.

DIRECTIONS: Questions 6 through 10 consist of four pairs of words each. Some of the words are spelled correctly; others are spelled incorrectly. For each question, indicate in the space at the right the letter preceding that pair of words in which BOTH words are spelled CORRECTLY.

6. A. hygienic, inviegle B. omniscience, pittance 6.____
   C. plagarize, nullify D. seargent, perilous

7. A. auxilary, existence B. pronounciation, accordance 7.____
   C. ignominy, indegence D. suable, baccalaureate

8. A. discreet, inaudible B. hypocrisy, currupt 8.____
   C. liquidate, maintainance D. transparancy, onerous

9. A. facility; stimulent B. frugel, sanitary 9.____
   C. monetary, prefatory D. punctileous, credentials

10. A. bankruptsy, perceptible B. disuade, resilient 10.____
    C. exhilerate, expectancy D. panegyric, disparate

Questions 11-15.

DIRECTIONS: Each question or incomplete statement is followed by several suggested answers or completions. Select the one that BEST answers the question or completes the statement. PRINT THE LETTER OF THE CORRECT ANSWER IN THE SPACE AT THE RIGHT.

11. The silent *e* must be retained when the suffix –*able* is added to the word
    A. argue B. love C. move D. notice

12. The CORRECTLY spelled word in the choices below is
    A. kindergarden
    B. zylophone
    C. hemorrhage
    D. mayonaise

13. Of the following words, the one spelled CORRECTLY is
    A. begger
    B. cemetary
    C. embarassed
    D. coyote

14.
    A. dandilion B. wiry C. sieze D. rythmic

15. A. beligerent
    B. anihilation
    C. facetious
    D. adversery

KEY (CORRECT ANSWERS)

1. B	6. B	11. D
2. C	7. D	12. C
3. D	8. A	13. D
4. A	9. C	14. B
5. D	10. D	15. C

TEST 8

DIRECTIONS: In each of the following sentences, one word is misspelled. Following each sentence is a list of four words taken from the sentence. Indicate the letter of the word which is MISSPELLED. *PRINT THE LETTER OF THE CORRECT ANSWER IN THE SPACE AT THE RIGHT.*

1. If the administrator attempts to withold information, there is a good likelihood that there will be serious repercussions.
   A. administrator
   B. withold
   C. likelihood
   D. repercussions

   1.____

2. He condescended to apologize, but we felt that a beligerent person should not occupy an influential position.
   A. condescended
   B. apologize
   C. beligerent
   D. influential

   2.____

3. Despite the sporadic delinquent payments of his indebtedness, Mr. Johnson has been an exemplery customer.
   A. sporadic
   B. delinquent
   C. indebtedness
   D. exemplery

   3.____

4. He was appreciative of the support he consistantly acquired, but he felt that he had waited an inordinate length of time for it.
   A. appreciative
   B. consistantly
   C. acquired
   D. inordinate

   4.____

5. Undeniably they benefited from the establishment of a receivership, but the question of statutary limitations remained unresolved.
   A. undeniably
   B. benefited
   C. receivership
   D. statutary

   5.____

6. Mr. Smith profered his hand as an indication that he considered it a viable contract, but Mr. Nelson alluded to the fact that his colleagues had not been consulted.
   A. profered
   B. viable
   C. alluded
   D. colleagues

   6.____

7. The treatments were beneficial according to the optomotrists, and the consensus was that minimal improvement could be expected.
   A. beneficial
   B. optomotrists
   C. consensus
   D. minimal

   7.____

8. Her frivolous manner was unbecoming because the air of solemnity at the cemetery was pervasive.
   A. frivalous
   B. solemnity
   C. cemetery
   D. pervasive

   8.____

9. The clandestine meetings were designed to make the two adversaries more amicable, but they served only to intensify their emnity.
   A. clandestine
   B. adversaries
   C. amicable
   D. emnity

   9._____

10. Do you think that his innovative ideas and financial acumen will help stabalize the fluctuations of the stock market?
    A. innovative
    B. acumen
    C. stabalize
    D. fluctuations

    10._____

11. In order to keep a perpetual inventory, you will have to keep an uninterrupted surveillance of all the miscellanious stock.
    A. perpetual
    B. uninterrupted
    C. surveillance
    D. miscellanious

    11._____

12. She used the art of pursuasion on the children because she found that caustic remarks had no perceptible effect on their behavior.
    A. pursuasion
    B. caustic
    C. perceptible
    D. effect

    12._____

13. His sacreligious outbursts offended his constituents, and he was summarily removed from office by the City Council.
    A. sacreligious
    B. constituents
    C. summarily
    D. Council

    13._____

14. They exhorted the contestants to greater efforts, but the exhorbitant costs in terms of energy expended resulted in a feeling of lethargy.
    A. exhorted
    B. contestants
    C. exhorbitant
    D. lethargy

    14._____

15. Since he was knowledgable about illicit drugs, he was served with a subpoena to appear for the prosecution.
    A. knowledgable
    B. illicit
    C. subpoena
    D. prosecution

    15._____

16. In spite of his lucid statements, they denigrated his report and decided it should be succintly paraphrased.
    A. lucid
    B. denigrated
    C. succintly
    D. paraphrased

    16._____

17. The discussion was not germane to the contraversy, but the indicted man's insistence on further talk was allowed.
    A. germane
    B. contraversy
    C. indicted
    D. insistence

    17._____

18. The legislators were enervated by the distances they had traveled during the election year to fullfil their speaking engagements.
    A. legislators
    B. enervated
    C. traveled
    D. fullfil

    18._____

19. The plaintiffs' attornies charge the defendant in the case with felonious assault. 19._____
    A. plaintiffs' B. attornies
    C. defendant D. felonious

20. It is symptomatic of the times that we try to placate all, but a proposal for new forms of disciplinery action was promulgated by the staff. 20._____
    A. symptomatic B. placate
    C. disciplinery D. promulgated

KEY (CORRECT ANSWERS)

1.	B	11.	D
2.	C	12.	A
3.	D	13.	A
4.	B	14.	C
5.	D	15.	A
6.	A	16.	C
7.	B	17.	B
8.	A	18.	D
9.	D	19.	B
10.	C	20.	C

TEST 9

DIRECTIONS: Each of Questions 1 through 15 consists of a single word which is spelled either correctly or incorrectly. If the word is spelled CORRECTLY, you are to print the letter C (Correct) in the space at the right. If the word is spelled INCORRECTL, you are to print the letter W (Wrong).

1. pospone 1.____
2. diffrent 2.____
3. height 3.____
4. carefully 4.____
5. ability 5.____
6. temper 6.____
7. deslike 7.____
8. seldem 8.____
9. alcohol 9.____
10. expense 10.____
11. vegatable 11.____
12. dispensary 12.____
13. specemin 13.____
14. allowance 14.____
15. exersise 15.____

KEY (CORRECT ANSWERS)

1.	W	6.	C	11.	W
2.	W	7.	W	12.	C
3.	C	8.	W	13.	W
4.	C	9.	C	14.	C
5.	C	10.	C	15.	W

TEST 10

DIRECTIONS: Each of Questions 1 through 10 consists of four words, one of which may be spelled incorrectly or all four words may be spelled correctly. If one of the words in a question is spelled incorrectly, print in the space at the right the capital letter preceding the word which is spelled INCORRECTLY. If all four words are spelled CORRECTLY, print the letter E.

1. A. dismissal   B. collateral   1.____
   C. leisure   D. proffession

2. A. subsidary   B. outrageous   2.____
   C. liaison   D. assessed

3. A. already   B. changeable   3.____
   C. mischevous   D. cylinder

4. A. supersede   B. deceit   4.____
   C. dissension   D. imminent

5. A. arguing   B. contagious   5.____
   C. comparitive   D. accessible

6. A. indelible   B. existance   6.____
   C. presumptuous   D. mileage

7. A. extention   B. aggregate   7.____
   C. sustenance   D. gratuitous

8. A. interrogate   B. exaggeration   8.____
   C. vacillate   D. moreover

9. A. parallel   B. derogatory   9.____
   C. admissible   D. appellate

10. A. safety   B. cumalative   10.____
    C. disappear   D. usable

KEY (CORRECT ANSWERS)

1.	D	6.	B
2.	A	7.	A
3.	C	8.	E
4.	E	9.	C
5.	C	10.	B

TEST 11

DIRECTIONS: Each of questions 1 through 10 consists of four words, one of which may be spelled incorrectly or all four words may be spelled correctly. If one of the words in a question is spelled INCORRECTLY, print in the space at the right the capital letter preceding the word which is spelled incorrectly. If all four words are spelled CORRECTLY, print the letter E.

1. A. vehicular B. gesticulate C. manageable D. fullfil 1.____

2. A. inovation B. onerous C. chastise D. irresistible 2.____

3. A. familiarize B. dissolution C. oscillate D. superflous 3.____

4. A. census B. defender C. adherence D. inconceivable 4.____

5. A. voluminous B. liberalize C. bankrupcy D. conversion 5.____

6. A. justifiable B. executor C. perpatrate D. dispelled 6.____

7. A. boycott B. abeyence C. enterprise D. circular 7.____

8. A. spontaineous B. dubious C. analyze D. premonition 8.____

9. A. intelligible B. apparently C. genuine D. crucial 9.____

10. A. plentiful B. ascertain C. carreer D. preliminary 10.____

KEY (CORRECT ANSWERS)

1. D   6. C
2. A   7. B
3. D   8. A
4. E   9. E
5. C   10. C

TEST 12

DIRECTIONS: Each of questions 1 through 25 consists of four words, one of which may be spelled incorrectly or all four words may be spelled correctly. If one of the words in a question is spelled INCORRECTLY, print in the space at the right the capital letter preceding the word which is spelled incorrectly. If all four words are spelled CORRECTLY, print the letter E.

1. A. temporary   B. existance
   C. complimentary   D. altogether   1._____

2. A. privilege   B. changeable
   C. jeopardize   D. commitment   2._____

3. A. grievous   B. alloted
   C. outrageous   D. mortgage   3._____

4. A. tempermental   B. accommodating
   C. bookkeeping   D. panicky   4._____

5. A. auxiliary   B. indispensable
   C. ecstasy   D. fiery   5._____

6. A. dissappear   B. buoyant
   C. imminent   D. parallel   6._____

7. A. loosly   B. medicine
   C. schedule   D. defendant   7._____

8. A. endeavor   B. persuade
   C. retroactive   D. desparate   8._____

9. A. usage   B. servicable
   C. disadvantageous   D. remittance   9._____

10. A. beneficary   B. receipt
    C. excitable   D. implement   10._____

11. A. accompanying   B. intangible
    C. offered   D. movable   11._____

12. A. controlling   B. seize
    C. repetitious   D. miscellaneous   12._____

13. A. installation   B. accommodation
    C. consistant   D. illuminate   13._____

14. A. incidentaly   B. privilege
    C. apparent   D. chargeable   14._____

116

2 (#12)

15. A. prevalent B. serial 15.____
C. briefly D. disatisfied

16. A. reciprocal B. concurrence 16.____
C. persistence D. withold

17. A. deferred B. suing 17.____
C. fulfilled D. pursuant

18. A. questionable B. omission 18.____
C. acknowledgment D. insistent

19. A. guarantee B. committment 19.____
C. mitigate D. publicly

20. A. prerogative B. apprise 20.____
C. extrordinary D. continual

21. A. arrogant B. handicapped 21.____
C. judicious D. perennial

22. A. permissable B. deceive 22.____
C. innumerable D. retrieve

23. A. notable B. allegiance 23.____
C. reimburse D. illegal

24. A. wholly B. disbursement 24.____
C. hindrance D. conciliatory

25. A. guidance B. condemn 25.____
C. publically D. coercion

KEY (CORRECT ANSWERS)

1.	B		11.	C
2.	E		12.	E
3.	B		13.	C
4.	A		14.	A
5.	E		15.	D
6.	A		16.	D
7.	A		17.	E
8.	D		18.	A
9.	B		19.	B
10.	A		20.	C

21. E
22. A
23. E
24. E
25. C

CLERICAL ABILITIES
EXAMINATION SECTION
TEST 1

DIRECTIONS: Each question or incomplete statement is followed by several suggested answers or completions. Select the one that BEST answers the question or completes the statement. *PRINT THE LETTER OF THE CORRECT ANSWER IN THE SPACE AT THE RIGHT.*

Questions 1-4.

DIRECTIONS: Questions 1 through 4 are to be answered on the basis of the information given below.

    The most commonly used filing system and the one that is easiest to learn is alphabetical filing. This involves putting records in an A to Z order, according to the letters of the alphabet. The name of a person is filed by using the following order: first, the surname or last name; second, the first name; third, the middle name or middle initial. For example, *Henry C. Young* is filed under *Y* and thereafter under *Young, Henry C.* The name of a company is filed in the same way. For example, *Long Cabinet Co.* is filed under *L* while *John T. Long Cabinet Co.* is filed under *L* and thereafter under *Long, John T. Cabinet Co.*

1. The one of the following which lists the names of persons in the CORRECT alphabetical order is:
   A. Mary Carrie, Helen Carrol, James Carson, John Carter
   B. James Carson, Mary Carrie, John Carter, Helen Carrol
   C. Helen Carrol, James Carson, John Carter, Mary Carrie
   D. John Carter, Helen Carrol, Mary Carrie, James Carson

    1.____

2. The one of the following which lists the names of persons in the CORRECT alphabetical order is:
   A. Jones, John C.; Jones, John A.; Jones, John P.; Jones, John K.
   B. Jones, John P.; Jones, John K.; Jones, John C.; Jones, John A.
   C. Jones, John A.; Jones, John C.; Jones, John K.; Jones, John P.
   D. Jones, John K.; Jones, John C.; Jones, John A.; Jones, John P.

    2.____

3. The one of the following which lists the names of the companies in the CORRECT alphabetical order is:
   A. Blane Co., Blake Co., Block Co., Blear Co.
   B. Blake Co., Blane Co., Blear Co., Block Co.
   C. Block Co., Blear Co., Blane Co., Blake Co.
   D. Blear Co., Blake Co., Blane Co., Block Co.

    3.____

4. You are to return to the file an index card on *Barry C. Wayne Materials and Supplies Co.*
Of the following, the CORRECT alphabetical group that you should return the index card to is
A. A to G   B. H to M   C. N to S   D. T to Z

Questions 5-10.

DIRECTIONS: In each of Questions 5 through 10, the names of four people are given. For each question, choose as your answer the one of the four names given which should be filed FIRST according to the usual system of alphabetical filing of names, as described in the following paragraph.

In filing names, you must start with the last name. Names are filed in order of the first letter of the last name, then the second letter, etc. Therefore, BAILY would be filed before BROWN, which would be filed before COLT. A name with fewer letters of the same type comes first, i.e., Smith before Smithe. If the last names are the same, the names are filed alphabetically by the first name. If the first name is an initial, a name with an initial would come before a first name that starts with the same letter as the initial. Therefore, I. BROWN would come before IRA BROWN. Finally, if both last name and first name are the same, the name would be filed alphabetically by the middle name, once again an initial coming before a middle name which starts with the same letter as the initial. If there is no middle name at all, the name would come before those with middle initials or names.

SAMPLE QUESTION:
A. Lester Daniels
B. William Dancer
C. Nathan Danzig
D. Dan Lester

The last names beginning with D are filed before the last name beginning with L. Since DANIELS, DANCER, and DANZIG all begin with the same three letters, you must look at the fourth letter of the last name to determine which name should be filed first. C comes before I or Z in the alphabet, so DANCER is filed before DANIELS or DANZIG. Therefore, the answer to the above sample question is B.

5. A. Scott Biala
    B. Mary Byala
    C. Martin Baylor
    D. Francis Bauer

6. A. Howard J. Black
    B. Howard Black
    C. J. Howard Black
    D. John H. Black

7. A. Theodora Garth Kingston
    B. Theadore Barth Kingston
    C. Thomas Kingston
    D. Thomas T. Kingston

8. A. Paulette Mary Huerta
    B. Paul M. Huerta
    C. Paulette L. Huerta
    D. Peter A. Huerta

9. A. Martha Hunt Morgan
    B. Martin Hunt Morgan
    C. Mary H. Morgan
    D. Martine H. Morgan

10. A. James T. Meerschaum
    B. James M. Mershum
    C. James F. Mearshaum
    D. James N. Meshum

Questions 11-14.

DIRECTIONS: Questions 11 through 14 are to be answered SOLELY on the basis of the following information.

You are required to file various documents in file drawers which are labeled according to the following pattern:

DOCUMENTS

MEMOS		LETTERS	
File	Subject	File	Subject
84PM1	(A-L)	84PC1	(A-L)
84PM2	(M-Z)	84PC2	(M-Z)

REPORTS		INQUIRIES	
File	Subject	File	Subject
84PR1	(A-L)	84PQ1	(A-L)
84PR2	(M-Z)	84PQ2	(M-Z)

11. A letter dealing with a burglary should be filed in the drawer labeled
    A. 84PM1   B. 84PC1   C. 84PR1   D. 84PQ2

12. A report on Statistics should be found in the drawer labeled
    A. 84PM1   B. 84PC2   C. 84PR2   D. 84PQS

13. An inquiry is received about parade permit procedures. It should be filed in the drawer labeled
    A. 84PM2   B. 84PC1   C. 84PR1   D. 84PQ2

14. A police officer has a question about a robbery report you filed. You should pull this file from the drawer labeled
    A. 84PM1   B. 84PM2   C. 84PR1   D. 84PR2

Questions 15-22.

DIRECTIONS: Each of Questions 15 through 22 consists of four or six numbered names. For each question, choose the option (A, B, C, or D) which indicates the order in which the names should be filed in accordance with the following filing instructions:
- File alphabetically according to last name, then first name, then middle initial.
- File according to each successive letter within a name.
- When comparing two names in which the letters in the longer name are identical to the corresponding letters in the shorter name, the shorter name is filed first.
- When the last names are the same, initials are always filed before names beginning with the same letter.

15. I. Ralph Robinson
    II. Alfred Ross
    III. Luis Robles
    IV. James Roberts

    The CORRECT filing sequence for the above names should be
    A. IV, II, I, III   B. I, IV, III, II   C. III, IV, I, II   D. IV, I, III, II

16. I. Irwin Goodwin
    II. Inez Gonzalez
    III. Irene Goodman
    IV. Ira S. Goodwin
    V. Ruth I. Goldstein
    VI. M.B. Goodman

    The CORRECT filing sequence for the above names should be
    A. V, II, I, IV, III, VI
    B. V, II, VI, III, IV, I
    C. V, II, III, VI, IV, I
    D. V, II, III, VI, I, IV

17. I. George Allan
    II. Gregory Allen
    III. Gary Allen
    IV. George Allen

    The CORRECT filing sequence for the above names should be
    A. IV, III, I, II   B. I, IV, II, III   C. III, IV, I, II   D. I, III, IV, II

18.
   I. Simon Kauffman
   II. Leo Kaufman
   III. Robert Kaufmann
   IV. Paul Kauffmann

   The CORRECT filing sequence for the above names should be
   A. I, IV, II, III   B. II, IV, III, I   C. III, II, IV, I   D. I, II, III, IV

   18.____

19.
   I. Roberta Williams
   II. Robin Wilson
   III. Roberta Wilson
   IV. Robin Williams

   The CORRECT filing sequence for the above names should be
   A. III, II, IV, I   B. I, IV, III, II   C. I, II, III, IV   D. III, I, II, IV

   19.____

20.
   I. Lawrence Shultz
   II. Albert Schultz
   III. Theodore Schwartz
   IV. Thomas Schwarz
   V. Alvin Schultz
   VI. Leonard Shultz

   The CORRECT filing sequence for the above names should be
   A. II, V, III, IV, I, VI   B. IV, III, V, I, II, VI
   C. II, V, I, VI, III, IV   D. I, VI, II, V, III, IV

   20.____

21.
   I. McArdle
   II. Mayer
   III. Maletz
   IV. McNiff
   V. Meyer
   VI. MacMahon

   The CORRECT filing sequence for the above names should be
   A. I, IV, VI, III, II, V   B. II, I, IV, VI, III, V
   C. VI, III, II, I, IV, V   D. VI, III, II, V, I, IV

   21.____

22.
   I. Jack E. Johnson
   II. R.H. Jackson
   III. Bertha Jackson
   IV. J.T. Johnson
   V. Ann Johns
   VI. John Jacobs

   The CORRECT filing sequence for the above names should be
   A. II, III, VI, V, IV, I   B. III, II, VI, V, IV, I
   C. VI, II, III, I, V, IV   D. III, II, VI, IV, V, I

   22.____

Questions 23-30.

DIRECTIONS: The code table below shows 10 letters with matching numbers. For each question, there are three sets of letters. Each set of letters is followed by a set of numbers which may or may not match their correct letter according to the code table. For each question, check all three sets of letters and numbers and mark your answer:
- A. if no pairs are correctly matched
- B. if only one pair is correctly matched
- C. if only two pairs are correctly matched
- D. if all three pairs are correctly matched

CODE TABLE

T	M	V	D	S	P	R	G	B	H
1	2	3	4	5	6	7	8	9	0

SAMPLE QUESTION: TMVDSP – 123456
RGBHTM – 789011
DSPRGB – 256789

In the sample question above, the first set of numbers correctly match its set of letters. But the second and third pairs contain mistakes. In the second pair, M is correctly matched with number 1. According to the code table, letter M should be correctly matched with number 2. In the third pair, the letter D is incorrectly matched with number 2. According to the code table, letter D should be correctly matched with number 4. Since only one of the pairs is correctly matched, the answer to this sample question is B.

23. RSBMRM – 759262
    GDSRVH – 845730
    VDBRTM - 349713   23.____

24. TGVSDR – 183247
    SMHRDP – 520647
    TRMHSR - 172057   24.____

25. DSPRGM – 456782
    MVDBHT – 234902
    HPMDBT - 062491   25.____

26. BVPTRD – 936184
    GDPHMB – 807029
    GMRHMV - 827032   26.____

27. MGVRSH – 283750
    TRDMBS – 174295
    SPRMGV - 567283   27.____

28. SGBSDM – 489542   28.____
    MGHPTM – 290612
    MPBMHT - 269301

29. TDPBHM – 146902   29.____
    VPBMRS – 369275
    GDMBHM - 842902

30. MVPTBV – 236194   30.____
    PDRTMB – 47128
    BGTMSM - 981232

KEY (CORRECT ANSWERS)

1. A	11. B	21. C
2. C	12. C	22. B
3. B	13. D	23. B
4. D	14. D	24. B
5. D	15. D	25. C
6. B	16. C	26. A
7. B	17. D	27. D
8. B	18. A	28. A
9. A	19. B	29. D
10. C	20. A	30. A

TEST 2

DIRECTIONS: Each question or incomplete statement is followed by several suggested answers or completions. Select the one that BEST answers the question or completes the statement. *PRINT THE LETTER OF THE CORRECT ANSWER IN THE SPACE AT THE RIGHT.*

Questions 1-10.

DIRECTIONS: Questions 1 through 10 each consists of two columns, each containing four lines of names, numbers and/or addresses. For each question, compare the lines in Column I with the lines in Column II to see if they match exactly, and mark your answer A, B, C, or D, according to the following instructions:
- A. all four lines match exactly
- B. only three lines match exactly
- C. only two lines match exactly
- D. only one line matches exactly

COLUMN I   COLUMN II

1. I.   Earl Hodgson   Earl Hodgson   1.____
    II. 1409870   1408970
    III. Shore Ave.   Schore Ave.
    IV. Macon Rd.   Macon Rd.

2. I.   9671485   9671485   2.____
    II. 470 Astor Court   470 Astor Court
    III. Halprin, Phillip   Halperin, Phillip
    IV. Frank D. Poliseo   Frank D. Poliseo

3. I.   Tandem Associates   Tandom Associates   3.____
    II. 144-17 Northern Blvd.   144-17 Northern Blvd.
    III. Alberta Forchi   Albert Forchi
    IV. Kings Park, NY 10751   Kings Point, NY 10751

4. I.   Bertha C. McCormack   Bertha C. McCormack   4.____
    II. Clayton, MO   Clayton, MO
    III. 976-4242   976-4242
    IV. New City, NY 10951   New City, NY 10951

5. I.   George C. Morill   George C. Morrill   5.____
    II. Columbia, SC 29201   Columbia, SD 29201
    III. Louis Ingham   Louis Ingham
    IV. 3406 Forest Ave.   3406 Forest Ave.

6. I.   506 S. Elliott Pl.   506 S. Elliott Pl.   6.____
    II. Herbert Hall   Hurbert Hall
    III. 4712 Rockaway Pkwy   4712 Rockaway Pkwy
    IV. 169 E. 7 St.   169 E. 7 St.

7.
   I. 345 Park Ave.   345 Park Pl.
   II. Colman Oven Corp.   Coleman Oven Corp.
   III. Robert Conte   Robert Conti
   IV. 6179846   6179846

7._____

8.
   I. Grigori Schierber   Grigori Schierber
   II. Des Moines, Iowa   Des Moines, Iowa
   III. Gouverneur Hospital Gouverneur Hospital
   IV. 91-35 Cresskill Pl.   91-35 Cresskill Pl.

8._____

9.
   I. Jeffery Janssen   Jeffrey Janssen
   II. 8041071   8041071
   III. 40 Rockefeller Plaza 40 Rockafeller Plaza
   IV. 407 6 St.   406 7 St.

9._____

10.
   I. 5971996   5871996
   II. 3113 Knickerbocker Ave.   31123 Knickerbocker Ave.
   III. 8434 Boston Post Rd.   8424 Boston Post Rd.
   IV. Penn Station   Penn Station

10._____

Questions 11-14.

DIRECTIONS: Questions 11 through 14 are to be answered by looking at the four groups of names and addresses listed below (I, II, III, and IV), and then finding out the number of groups that have their corresponding numbered lies exactly the same.

	GROUP I	GROUP II
Line 1.	Richmond General Hospital	Richman General Hospital
Line 2.	Geriatric Clinic	Geriatric Clinic
Line 3.	3975 Paerdegat St.	3975 Peardegat St.
Line 4.	Loudonville, New York 11538	Londonville, New York 11538

	GROUP III	GROUP IV
Line 1.	Richmond General Hospital	Richmend General Hospital
Line 2.	Geriatric Clinic	Geriatric Clinic
Line 3.	3795 Paerdegat St.	3975 Paerdegat St.
Line 4.	Loudonville, New York 11358	Loudonville, New York 11538

1. In how many groups is line one exactly the same?
   A. Two   B. Three   C. Four   D. None

11._____

12. In how many groups is line two exactly the same?
   A. Two   B. Three   C. Four   D. None

12._____

13. In how many groups is line three exactly the same?
   A. Two   B. Three   C. Four   D. None

13._____

14. In how many groups is line four exactly the same? 14._____
    A. Two   B. Three   C. Four   D. None

Questions 15-18.

DIRECTIONS: Each of Questions 15 through 18 has two lists of names and addresses. Each list contains three sets of names and addresses. Check each of the three sets in the list on the right to see if they are the same as the corresponding set in the list on the left. Mark your answers:
   A. if none of the sets in the right list are the same as those in the left list
   B. if only one of the sets in the right list is the same as those in the left list
   C. if only two of the sets in the right list are the same as those in the left list
   D. if all three sets in the right list are the same as those in the left list

15. Mary T. Berlinger
    2351 Hampton St.
    Monsey, N.Y. 20117

    Eduardo Benes
    483 Kingston Avenue
    Central Islip, N.Y. 11734

    Alan Carrington Fuchs
    17 Gnarled Hollow Road
    Los Angeles, CA 91635

    Mary T. Berlinger
    2351 Hampton St.
    Monsey, N.Y. 20117

    Eduardo Benes
    473 Kingston Avenue
    Central Islip, N.Y. 11734

    Alan Carrington Fuchs
    17 Gnarled Hollow Road
    Los Angeles, CA 91685

    15._____

16. David John Jacobson
    178 34 St. Apt. 4C
    New York, N.Y. 00927

    Ann-Marie Calonella
    7243 South Ridge Blvd.
    Bakersfield, CA 96714

    Pauline M. Thompson
    872 Linden Ave.
    Houston, Texas 70321

    David John Jacobson
    178 53 St. Apt. 4C
    New York, N.Y. 00927

    Ann-Marie Calonella
    7243 South Ridge Blvd.
    Bakersfield, CA 96714

    Pauline M. Thomson
    872 Linden Ave.
    Houston, Texas 70321

    16._____

17. Chester LeRoy Masterton
    152 Lacy Rd.
    Kankakee, Ill. 54532

    William Maloney
    S. LaCrosse Pla.
    Wausau, Wisconsin 52136

    Cynthia V. Barnes
    16 Pines Rd.
    Greenpoint, Miss. 20376

    Chester LeRoy Masterson
    152 Lacy Rd.
    Kankakee, Ill. 54532

    William Maloney
    S. LaCross Pla.
    Wausau, Wisconsin 52146

    Cynthia V. Barnes
    16 Pines Rd.
    Greenpoint,, Miss. 20376

    17._____

4 (#2)

18. Marcel Jean Frontenac
8 Burton On The Water
Calender, Me. 01471

Marcel Jean Frontenac
6 Burton On The Water
Calender, Me. 01471

18._____

J. Scott Marsden
174 S. Tipton St.
Cleveland, Ohio

J. Scott Marsden
174 Tipton St.
Cleveland, Ohio

Lawrence T. Haney
171 McDonough St.
Decatur, Ga. 31304

Lawrence T. Haney
171 McDonough St.
Decatur, Ga. 31304

Questions 19-26.

DIRECTIONS: Each of Questions 19 through 26 has two lists of numbers. Each list contains three sets of numbers. Check each of the three sets in the list on the right to see if they are the same as the corresponding set in the list on the left. Mark your answers:
- A. if none of the sets in the right list are the same as those in the left list
- B. if only one of the sets in the right list is the same as those in the left list
- C. if only two of the sets in the right list are the same as those in the left list
- D. if all three sets in the right list are the same as those in the left lists

19. 7354183476
4474747744
5791430231

7354983476
4474747774
57914302311

19._____

20. 7143592185
8344517699
9178531263

7143892185
8344518699
9178531263

20._____

21. 2572114731
8806835476
8255831246

257214731
8806835476
8255831246

21._____

22. 331476853821
6976658532996
3766042113715

331476858621
6976655832996
3766042113745

22._____

23. 8806663315
74477138449
211756663666

88066633115
74477138449
211756663666

23._____

129

24. 990006966996   99000696996   24.____
    53022219743   53022219843
    4171171117717   4171171177717

25. 24400222433004   24400222433004   25.____
    5300030055000355   5300030055500355
    20000075532002022 20000075532002022

26. 611166640660001116   61116664066001116   26.____
    7111300117001100733   7111300117001100733
    26666446664476518   26666446664476518

Questions 27-30.

DIRECTIONS: Questions 27 through 30 are to be answered by picking the answer which is in the correct numerical order, from the lowest number to the highest number, in each question.

27. A. 44533, 44518, 44516, 44547   27.____
    B. 44516, 44518, 44533, 44547
    C. 44547, 44533, 44518, 44516
    D. 44518, 44516, 44547, 44533

28. A. 95587, 95593, 95601, 95620   28.____
    B. 95601, 95620, 95587, 95593
    C. 95593, 95587, 95601. 95620
    D. 95620, 95601, 95593, 95587

29. A. 232212, 232208, 232232, 232223   29.____
    B. 232208, 232223, 232212, 232232
    C. 232208, 232212, 232223, 232232
    D. 232223, 232232, 232208, 232208

30. A. 113419, 113521, 113462, 113462   30.____
    B. 113588, 113462, 113521, 113419
    C. 113521, 113588, 113419, 113462
    D. 113419, 113462, 113521, 113588

KEY (CORRECT ANSWERS)

1.	C	11.	A	21.	C
2.	B	12.	C	22.	A
3.	D	13.	A	23.	D
4.	A	14.	A	24.	A
5.	C	15.	C	25.	C
6.	B	16.	B	26.	C
7.	D	17.	B	27.	B
8.	A	18.	B	28.	A
9.	D	19.	B	29.	C
10.	C	20.	B	30.	D

GLOSSARY OF LEGAL TERMS

TABLE OF CONTENTS

	Page
Action ... Affiant	1
Affidavit ... At Bar	2
At Issue ... Burden of Proof	3
Business ... Commute	4
Complainant ... Conviction	5
Cooperative ... Demur (v.)	6
Demurrage ... Endorsement	7
Enjoin ... Facsimile	8
Factor ... Guilty	9
Habeas Corpus ... Incumbrance	10
Indemnify ... Laches	11
Landlord and Tenant ... Malice	12
Mandamus ... Obiter Dictum	13
Object (v.) ... Perjury	14
Perpetuity ... Proclamation	15
Proffered Evidence ... Referee	16
Referendum ... Stare Decisis	17
State ... Term	18
Testamentary ... Warrant (Warranty) (v.)	19
Warrant (n.) ... Zoning	20

GLOSSARY OF LEGAL TERMS

A

ACTION - "Action" includes a civil action and a criminal action.

A FORTIORI - A term meaning you can reason one thing from the existence of certain facts.

A POSTERIORI - From what goes after; from effect to cause.

A PRIORI - From what goes before; from cause to effect.

AB INITIO - From the beginning.

ABATE - To diminish or put an end to.

ABET - To encourage the commission of a crime.

ABEYANCE - Suspension, temporary suppression.

ABIDE - To accept the consequences of.

ABJURE - To renounce; give up.

ABRIDGE - To reduce; contract; diminish.

ABROGATE - To annul, repeal, or destroy.

ABSCOND - To hide or absent oneself to avoid legal action.

ABSTRACT - A summary.

ABUT - To border on, to touch.

ACCESS - Approach; in real property law it means the right of the owner of property to the use of the highway or road next to his land, without obstruction by intervening property owners.

ACCESSORY - In criminal law, it means the person who contributes or aids in the commission of a crime.

ACCOMMODATED PARTY - One to whom credit is extended on the strength of another person signing a commercial paper.

ACCOMMODATION PAPER - A commercial paper to which the accommodating party has put his name.

ACCOMPLICE - In criminal law, it means a person who together with the principal offender commits a crime.

ACCORD - An agreement to accept something different or less than that to which one is entitled, which extinguishes the entire obligation.

ACCOUNT - A statement of mutual demands in the nature of debt and credit between parties.

ACCRETION - The act of adding to a thing; in real property law, it means gradual accumulation of land by natural causes.

ACCRUE - To grow to; to be added to.

ACKNOWLEDGMENT - The act of going before an official authorized to take acknowledgments, and acknowledging an act as one's own.

ACQUIESCENCE - A silent appearance of consent.

ACQUIT - To legally determine the innocence of one charged with a crime.

AD INFINITUM - Indefinitely.

AD LITEM - For the suit.

AD VALOREM - According to value.

ADJECTIVE LAW - Rules of procedure.

ADJUDICATION - The judgment given in a case.

ADMIRALTY - Court having jurisdiction over maritime cases.

ADULT - Sixteen years old or over (in criminal law).

ADVANCE - In commercial law, it means to pay money or render other value before it is due.

ADVERSE - Opposed; contrary.

ADVOCATE - (v.) To speak in favor of;
(n.) One who assists, defends, or pleads for another.

AFFIANT - A person who makes and signs an affidavit.

AFFIDAVIT - A written and sworn to declaration of facts, voluntarily made.

AFFINITY - The relationship between persons through marriage with the kindred of each other; distinguished from consanguinity, which is the relationship by blood.

AFFIRM - To ratify; also when an appellate court affirms a judgment, decree, or order, it means that it is valid and right and must stand as rendered in the lower court.

AFOREMENTIONED; AFORESAID - Before or already said.

AGENT - One who represents and acts for another.

AID AND COMFORT - To help; encourage.

ALIAS - A name not one's true name.

ALIBI - A claim of not being present at a certain place at a certain time.

ALLEGE - To assert.

ALLOTMENT - A share or portion.

AMBIGUITY - Uncertainty; capable of being understood in more than one way.

AMENDMENT - Any language made or proposed as a change in some principal writing.

AMICUS CURIAE - A friend of the court; one who has an interest in a case, although not a party in the case, who volunteers advice upon matters of law to the judge. For example, a brief amicus curiae.

AMORTIZATION - To provide for a gradual extinction of (a future obligation) in advance of maturity, especially, by periodical contributions to a sinking fund which will be adequate to discharge a debt or make a replacement when it becomes necessary.

ANCILLARY - Aiding, auxiliary.

ANNOTATION - A note added by way of comment or explanation.

ANSWER - A written statement made by a defendant setting forth the grounds of his defense.

ANTE - Before.

ANTE MORTEM - Before death.

APPEAL - The removal of a case from a lower court to one of superior jurisdiction for the purpose of obtaining a review.

APPEARANCE - Coming into court as a party to a suit.

APPELLANT - The party who takes an appeal from one court or jurisdiction to another (appellate) court for review.

APPELLEE - The party against whom an appeal is taken.

APPROPRIATE - To make a thing one's own.

APPROPRIATION - Prescribing the destination of a thing; the act of the legislature designating a particular fund, to be applied to some object of government expenditure.

APPURTENANT - Belonging to; accessory or incident to.

ARBITER - One who decides a dispute; a referee.

ARBITRARY - Unreasoned; not governed by any fixed rules or standard.

ARGUENDO - By way of argument.

ARRAIGN - To call the prisoner before the court to answer to a charge.

ASSENT - A declaration of willingness to do something in compliance with a request.

ASSERT - Declare.

ASSESS - To fix the rate or amount.

ASSIGN - To transfer; to appoint; to select for a particular purpose.

ASSIGNEE - One who receives an assignment.

ASSIGNOR - One who makes an assignment.

AT BAR - Before the court.

AT ISSUE - When parties in an action come to a point where one asserts something and the other denies it.
ATTACH - Seize property by court order and sometimes arrest a person.
ATTEST - To witness a will, etc.; act of attestation.
AVERMENT - A positive statement of facts.

B

BAIL - To obtain the release of a person from legal custody by giving security and promising that he shall appear in court; to deliver (goods, etc.) in trust to a person for a special purpose.
BAILEE - One to whom personal property is delivered under a contract of bailment.
BAILMENT - Delivery of personal property to another to be held for a certain purpose and to be returned when the purpose is accomplished.
BAILOR - The party who delivers goods to another, under a contract of bailment.
BANC (OR BANK) - Bench; the place where a court sits permanently or regularly; also the assembly of all the judges of a court.
BANKRUPT - An insolvent person, technically, one declared to be bankrupt after a bankruptcy proceeding.
BAR - The legal profession.
BARRATRY - Exciting groundless judicial proceedings.
BARTER - A contract by which parties exchange goods for other goods.
BATTERY - Illegal interfering with another's person.
BEARER - In commercial law, it means the person in possession of a commercial paper which is payable to the bearer.
BENCH - The court itself or the judge.
BENEFICIARY - A person benefiting under a will, trust, or agreement.
BEST EVIDENCE RULE, THE - Except as otherwise provided by statute, no evidence other than the writing itself is admissible to prove the content of a writing. This section shall be known and may be cited as the best evidence rule.
BEQUEST - A gift of personal property under a will.
BILL - A formal written statement of complaint to a court of justice; also, a draft of an act of the legislature before it becomes a law; also, accounts for goods sold, services rendered, or work done.
BONA FIDE - In or with good faith; honestly.
BOND - An instrument by which the maker promises to pay a sum of money to another, usually providing that upon performances of a certain condition the obligation shall be void.
BOYCOTT - A plan to prevent the carrying on of a business by wrongful means.
BREACH - The breaking or violating of a law, or the failure to carry out a duty.
BRIEF - A written document, prepared by a lawyer to serve as the basis of an argument upon a case in court, usually an appellate court.
BURDEN OF PRODUCING EVIDENCE - The obligation of a party to introduce evidence sufficient to avoid a ruling against him on the issue.
BURDEN OF PROOF - The obligation of a party to establish by evidence a requisite degree of belief concerning a fact in the mind of the trier of fact or the court. The burden of proof may require a party to raise a reasonable doubt concerning the existence of nonexistence of a fact or that he establish the existence or nonexistence of a fact by a preponderance of the evidence, by clear and convincing proof, or by proof beyond a reasonable doubt.

Except as otherwise provided by law, the burden of proof requires proof by a preponderance of the evidence.

BUSINESS, A - Shall include every kind of business, profession, occupation, calling or operation of institutions, whether carried on for profit or not.

BY-LAWS - Regulations, ordinances, or rules enacted by a corporation, association, etc., for its own government.

C

CANON - A doctrine; also, a law or rule, of a church or association in particular.

CAPIAS - An order to arrest.

CAPTION - In a pleading, deposition or other paper connected with a case in court, it is the heading or introductory clause which shows the names of the parties, name of the court, number of the case on the docket or calendar, etc.

CARRIER - A person or corporation undertaking to transport persons or property.

CASE - A general term for an action, cause, suit, or controversy before a judicial body.

CAUSE - A suit, litigation or action before a court.

CAVEAT EMPTOR - Let the buyer beware. This term expresses the rule that the purchaser of an article must examine, judge, and test it for himself, being bound to discover any obvious defects or imperfections.

CERTIFICATE - A written representation that some legal formality has been complied with.

CERTIORARI - To be informed of; the name of a writ issued by a superior court directing the lower court to send up to the former the record and proceedings of a case.

CHANGE OF VENUE - To remove place of trial from one place to another.

CHARGE - An obligation or duty; a formal complaint; an instruction of the court to the jury upon a case.

CHARTER - (n.) The authority by virtue of which an organized body acts;
    (v.) in mercantile law, it means to hire or lease a vehicle or vessel for transportation.

CHATTEL - An article of personal property.

CHATTEL MORTGAGE - A mortgage on personal property.

CIRCUIT - A division of the country, for the administration of justice; a geographical area served by a court.

CITATION - The act of the court by which a person is summoned or cited; also, a reference to legal authority.

CIVIL (ACTIONS)- It indicates the private rights and remedies of individuals in contrast to the word "criminal" (actions) which relates to prosecution for violation of laws.

CLAIM (n.) - Any demand held or asserted as of right.

CODICIL - An addition to a will.

CODIFY - To arrange the laws of a country into a code.

COGNIZANCE - Notice or knowledge.

COLLATERAL - By the side; accompanying; an article or thing given to secure performance of a promise.

COMITY - Courtesy; the practice by which one court follows the decision of another court on the same question.

COMMIT - To perform, as an act; to perpetrate, as a crime; to send a person to prison.

COMMON LAW - As distinguished from law created by the enactment of the legislature (called statutory law), it relates to those principles and rules of action which derive their authority solely from usages and customs of immemorial antiquity, particularly with reference to the ancient unwritten law of England. The written pronouncements of the common law are found in court decisions.

COMMUTE - Change punishment to one less severe.

COMPLAINANT - One who applies to the court for legal redress.
COMPLAINT - The pleading of a plaintiff in a civil action; or a charge that a person has committed a specified offense.
COMPROMISE - An arrangement for settling a dispute by agreement.
CONCUR - To agree, consent.
CONCURRENT - Running together, at the same time.
CONDEMNATION - Taking private property for public use on payment therefor.
CONDITION - Mode or state of being; a qualification or restriction.
CONDUCT - Active and passive behavior; both verbal and nonverbal.
CONFESSION - Voluntary statement of guilt of crime.
CONFIDENTIAL COMMUNICATION BETWEEN CLIENT AND LAWYER - Information transmitted between a client and his lawyer in the course of that relationship and in confidence by a means which, so far as the client is aware, discloses the information to no third persons other than those who are present to further the interest of the client in the consultation or those to whom disclosure is reasonably necessary for the transmission of the information or the accomplishment of the purpose for which the lawyer is consulted, and includes a legal opinion formed and the advice given by the lawyer in the course of that relationship.
CONFRONTATION - Witness testifying in presence of defendant.
CONSANGUINITY - Blood relationship.
CONSIGN - To give in charge; commit; entrust; to send or transmit goods to a merchant, factor, or agent for sale.
CONSIGNEE - One to whom a consignment is made.
CONSIGNOR - One who sends or makes a consignment.
CONSPIRACY - In criminal law, it means an agreement between two or more persons to commit an unlawful act.
CONSPIRATORS - Persons involved in a conspiracy.
CONSTITUTION - The fundamental law of a nation or state.
CONSTRUCTION OF GENDERS - The masculine gender includes the feminine and neuter.
CONSTRUCTION OF SINGULAR AND PLURAL - The singular number includes the plural; and the plural, the singular.
CONSTRUCTION OF TENSES - The present tense includes the past and future tenses; and the future, the present.
CONSTRUCTIVE - An act or condition assumed from other parts or conditions.
CONSTRUE - To ascertain the meaning of language.
CONSUMMATE - To complete.
CONTIGUOUS - Adjoining; touching; bounded by.
CONTINGENT - Possible, but not assured; dependent upon some condition.
CONTINUANCE - The adjournment or postponement of an action pending in a court.
CONTRA - Against, opposed to; contrary.
CONTRACT - An agreement between two or more persons to do or not to do a particular thing.
CONTROVERT - To dispute, deny.
CONVERSION - Dealing with the personal property of another as if it were one's own, without right.
CONVEYANCE - An instrument transferring title to land.
CONVICTION - Generally, the result of a criminal trial which ends in a judgment or sentence that the defendant is guilty as charged.

COOPERATIVE - A cooperative is a voluntary organization of persons with a common interest, formed and operated along democratic lines for the purpose of supplying services at cost to its members and other patrons, who contribute both capital and business.
CORPUS DELICTI - The body of a crime; the crime itself.
CORROBORATE - To strengthen; to add weight by additional evidence.
COUNTERCLAIM - A claim presented by a defendant in opposition to or deduction from the claim of the plaintiff.
COUNTY - Political subdivision of a state.
COVENANT - Agreement.
CREDIBLE - Worthy of belief.
CREDITOR - A person to whom a debt is owing by another person, called the "debtor."
CRIMINAL ACTION - Includes criminal proceedings.
CRIMINAL INFORMATION - Same as complaint.
CRITERION (sing.)
CRITERIA (plural) - A means or tests for judging; a standard or standards.
CROSS-EXAMINATION - Examination of a witness by a party other than the direct examiner upon a matter that is within the scope of the direct examination of the witness.
CULPABLE - Blamable.
CY-PRES - As near as (possible). The rule of *cy-pres* is a rule for the construction of instruments in equity by which the intention of the party is carried out *as near as may be*, when it would be impossible or illegal to give it literal effect.

D

DAMAGES - A monetary compensation, which may be recovered in the courts by any person who has suffered loss, or injury, whether to his person, property or rights through the unlawful act or omission or negligence of another.
DECLARANT - A person who makes a statement.
DE FACTO - In fact; actually but without legal authority.
DE JURE - Of right; legitimate; lawful.
DE MINIMIS - Very small or trifling.
DE NOVO - Anew; afresh; a second time.
DEBT - A specified sum of money owing to one person from another, including not only the obligation of the debtor to pay, but the right of the creditor to receive and enforce payment.
DECEDENT - A dead person.
DECISION - A judgment or decree pronounced by a court in determination of a case.
DECREE - An order of the court, determining the rights of all parties to a suit.
DEED - A writing containing a contract sealed and delivered; particularly to convey real property.
DEFALCATION - Misappropriation of funds.
DEFAMATION - Injuring one's reputation by false statements.
DEFAULT - The failure to fulfill a duty, observe a promise, discharge an obligation, or perform an agreement.
DEFENDANT - The person defending or denying; the party against whom relief or recovery is sought in an action or suit.
DEFRAUD - To practice fraud; to cheat or trick.
DELEGATE (v.)- To entrust to the care or management of another.
DELICTUS - A crime.
DEMUR (v.) - To dispute the sufficiency in law of the pleading of the other side.

DEMURRAGE - In maritime law, it means, the sum fixed or allowed as remuneration to the owners of a ship for the detention of their vessel beyond the number of days allowed for loading and unloading or for sailing; also used in railroad terminology.
DENIAL - A form of pleading; refusing to admit the truth of a statement, charge, etc.
DEPONENT - One who gives testimony under oath reduced to writing.
DEPOSITION - Testimony given under oath outside of court for use in court or for the purpose of obtaining information in preparation for trial of a case.
DETERIORATION - A degeneration such as from decay, corrosion or disintegration.
DETRIMENT - Any loss or harm to person or property.
DEVIATION - A turning aside.
DEVISE - A gift of real property by the last will and testament of the donor.
DICTUM (sing.)
DICTA (plural) - Any statements made by the court in an opinion concerning some rule of law not necessarily involved nor essential to the determination of the case.
DIRECT EVIDENCE - Evidence that directly proves a fact, without an inference or presumption, and which in itself if true, conclusively establishes that fact.
DIRECT EXAMINATION - The first examination of a witness upon a matter that is not within the scope of a previous examination of the witness.
DISAFFIRM - To repudiate.
DISMISS - In an action or suit, it means to dispose of the case without any further consideration or hearing.
DISSENT - To denote disagreement of one or more judges of a court with the decision passed by the majority upon a case before them.
DOCKET (n.) - A formal record, entered in brief, of the proceedings in a court.
DOCTRINE - A rule, principle, theory of law.
DOMICILE - That place where a man has his true, fixed and permanent home to which whenever he is absent he has the intention of returning.
DRAFT (n.) - A commercial paper ordering payment of money drawn by one person on another.
DRAWEE - The person who is requested to pay the money.
DRAWER - The person who draws the commercial paper and addresses it to the drawee.
DUPLICATE - A counterpart produced by the same impression as the original enlargements and miniatures, or by mechanical or electronic re-recording, or by chemical reproduction, or by other equivalent technique which accurately reproduces the original.
DURESS - Use of force to compel performance or non-performance of an act.

E

EASEMENT - A liberty, privilege, or advantage without profit, in the lands of another.
EGRESS - Act or right of going out or leaving; emergence.
EIUSDEM GENERIS - Of the same kind, class or nature. A rule used in the construction of language in a legal document.
EMBEZZLEMENT - To steal; to appropriate fraudulently to one's own use property entrusted to one's care.
EMBRACERY - Unlawful attempt to influence jurors, etc., but not by offering value.
EMINENT DOMAIN - The right of a state to take private property for public use.
ENACT - To make into a law.
ENDORSEMENT - Act of writing one's name on the back of a note, bill or similar written instrument.

ENJOIN - To require a person, by writ of injunction from a court of equity, to perform or to abstain or desist from some act.
ENTIRETY - The whole; that which the law considers as one whole, and not capable of being divided into parts.
ENTRAPMENT - Inducing one to commit a crime so as to arrest him.
ENUMERATED - Mentioned specifically; designated.
ENURE - To operate or take effect.
EQUITY - In its broadest sense, this term denotes the spirit and the habit of fairness, justness, and right dealing which regulate the conduct of men.
ERROR - A mistake of law, or the false or irregular application of law as will nullify the judicial proceedings.
ESCROW - A deed, bond or other written engagement, delivered to a third person, to be delivered by him only upon the performance or fulfillment of some condition.
ESTATE - The interest which any one has in lands, or in any other subject of property.
ESTOP - To stop, bar, or impede.
ESTOPPEL - A rule of law which prevents a man from alleging or denying a fact, because of his own previous act.
ET AL. (alii) - And others.
ET SEQ. (sequential) - And the following.
ET UX. (uxor) - And wife.
EVIDENCE - Testimony, writings, material objects, or other things presented to the senses that are offered to prove the existence or non-existence of a fact.
  Means from which inferences may be drawn as a basis of proof in duly constituted judicial or fact finding tribunals, and includes testimony in the form of opinion and hearsay.
EX CONTRACTU
EX DELICTO - In law, rights and causes of action are divided into two classes, those arising *ex contractu* (from a contract) and those arising *ex delicto* (from a delict or tort).
EX OFFICIO - From office; by virtue of the office.
EX PARTE - On one side only; by or for one.
EX POST FACTO - After the fact.
EX POST FACTO LAW - A law passed after an act was done which retroactively makes such act a crime.
EX REL. (relations) - Upon relation or information.
EXCEPTION - An objection upon a matter of law to a decision made, either before or after judgment by a court.
EXECUTOR (male)
EXECUTRIX (female) - A person who has been appointed by will to execute the will.
EXECUTORY - That which is yet to be executed or performed.
EXEMPT - To release from some liability to which others are subject.
EXONERATION - The removal of a burden, charge or duty.
EXTRADITION - Surrender of a fugitive from one nation to another.

F

F.A.S.- "Free alongside ship"; delivery at dock for ship named.
F.O.B.- "Free on board"; seller will deliver to car, truck, vessel, or other conveyance by which goods are to be transported, without expense or risk of loss to the buyer or consignee.
FABRICATE - To construct; to invent a false story.
FACSIMILE - An exact or accurate copy of an original instrument.

FACTOR - A commercial agent.
FEASANCE - The doing of an act.
FELONIOUS - Criminal, malicious.
FELONY - Generally, a criminal offense that may be punished by death or imprisonment for more than one year as differentiated from a misdemeanor.
FEME SOLE - A single woman.
FIDUCIARY - A person who is invested with rights and powers to be exercised for the benefit of another person.
FIERI FACIAS - A writ of execution commanding the sheriff to levy and collect the amount of a judgment from the goods and chattels of the judgment debtor.
FINDING OF FACT - Determination from proof or judicial notice of the existence of a fact. A ruling implies a supporting finding of fact; no separate or formal finding is required unless required by a statute of this state.
FISCAL - Relating to accounts or the management of revenue.
FORECLOSURE (sale) - A sale of mortgaged property to obtain satisfaction of the mortgage out of the sale proceeds.
FORFEITURE - A penalty, a fine.
FORGERY - Fabricating or producing falsely, counterfeited.
FORTUITOUS - Accidental.
FORUM - A court of justice; a place of jurisdiction.
FRAUD - Deception; trickery.
FREEHOLDER - One who owns real property.
FUNGIBLE - Of such kind or nature that one specimen or part may be used in the place of another.

G

GARNISHEE - Person garnished.
GARNISHMENT - A legal process to reach the money or effects of a defendant, in the possession or control of a third person.
GRAND JURY - Not less than 16, not more than 23 citizens of a county sworn to inquire into crimes committed or triable in the county.
GRANT - To agree to; convey, especially real property.
GRANTEE - The person to whom a grant is made.
GRANTOR - The person by whom a grant is made.
GRATUITOUS - Given without a return, compensation or consideration.
GRAVAMEN - The grievance complained of or the substantial cause of a criminal action.
GUARANTY (n.) - A promise to answer for the payment of some debt, or the performance of some duty, in case of the failure of another person, who, in the first instance, is liable for such payment or performance.
GUARDIAN - The person, committee, or other representative authorized by law to protect the person or estate or both of an incompetent (or of a *sui juris* person having a guardian) and to act for him in matters affecting his person or property or both. An incompetent is a person under disability imposed by law.
GUILTY - Establishment of the fact that one has committed a breach of conduct; especially, a violation of law.

H

HABEAS CORPUS - You have the body; the name given to a variety of writs, having for their object to bring a party before a court or judge for decision as to whether such person is being lawfully held prisoner.
HABENDUM - In conveyancing; it is the clause in a deed conveying land which defines the extent of ownership to be held by the grantee.
HEARING - A proceeding whereby the arguments of the interested parties are heared.
HEARSAY - A type of testimony given by a witness who relates, not what he knows personally, but what others have told hi, or what he has heard said by others.
HEARSAY RULE, THE - (a) "Hearsay evidence" is evidence of a statement that was made other than by a witness while testifying at the hearing and that is offered to prove the truth of the matter stated; (b) Except as provided by law, hearsay evidence is inadmissible; (c) This section shall be known and may be cited as the hearsay rule.
HEIR - Generally, one who inherits property, real or personal.
HOLDER OF THE PRIVILEGE - (a) The client when he has no guardian or conservator; (b) A guardian or conservator of the client when the client has a guardian or conservator; (c) The personal representative of the client if the client is dead; (d) A successor, assign, trustee in dissolution, or any similar representative of a firm, association, organization, partnership, business trust, corporation, or public entity that is no longer in existence.
HUNG JURY - One so divided that they can't agree on a verdict.
HUSBAND-WIFE PRIVILEGE - An accused in a criminal proceeding has a privilege to prevent his spouse from testifying against him.
HYPOTHECATE - To pledge a thing without delivering it to the pledgee.
HYPOTHESIS - A supposition, assumption, or toehry.

I

I.E. (id est) - That is.
IB., OR IBID.(ibidem) - In the same place; used to refer to a legal reference previously cited to avoid repeating the entire citation.
ILLICIT - Prohibited; unlawful.
ILLUSORY - Deceiving by false appearance.
IMMUNITY - Exemption.
IMPEACH - To accuse, to dispute.
IMPEDIMENTS - Disabilities, or hindrances.
IMPLEAD - To sue or prosecute by due course of law.
IMPUTED - Attributed or charged to.
IN LOCO PARENTIS - In place of parent, a guardian.
IN TOTO - In the whole; completely.
INCHOATE - Imperfect; unfinished.
INCOMMUNICADO - Denial of the right of a prisoner to communicate with friends or relatives.
INCOMPETENT - One who is incapable of caring for his own affairs because he is mentally deficient or undeveloped.
INCRIMINATION - A matter will incriminate a person if it constitutes, or forms an essential part of, or, taken in connection with other matters disclosed, is a basis for a reasonable inference of such a violation of the laws of this State as to subject him to liability to punishment therefor, unless he has become for any reason permanently immune from punishment for such violation.
INCUMBRANCE - Generally a claim, lien, charge or liability attached to and binding real property.

INDEMNIFY - To secure against loss or damage; also, to make reimbursement to one for a loss already incurred by him.
INDEMNITY - An agreement to reimburse another person in case of an anticipated loss falling upon him.
INDICIA - Signs; indications.
INDICTMENT - An accusation in writing found and presented by a grand jury charging that a person has committed a crime.
INDORSE - To write a name on the back of a legal paper or document, generally, a negotiable instrument
INDUCEMENT - Cause or reason why a thing is done or that which incites the person to do the act or commit a crime; the motive for the criminal act.
INFANT - In civil cases one under 21 years of age.
INFORMATION - A formal accusation of crime made by a prosecuting attorney.
INFRA - Below, under; this word occurring by itself in a publication refers the reader to a future part of the publication.
INGRESS - The act of going into.
INJUNCTION - A writ or order by the court requiring a person, generally, to do or to refrain from doing an act.
INSOLVENT - The condition of a person who is unable to pay his debts.
INSTRUCTION - A direction given by the judge to the jury concerning the law of the case.
INTERIM - In the meantime; time intervening.
INTERLOCUTORY - Temporary, not final; something intervening between the commencement and the end of a suit which decides some point or matter, but is not a final decision of the whole controversy.
INTERROGATORIES - A series of formal written questions used in the examination of a party or a witness usually prior to a trial.
INTESTATE - A person who dies without a will.
INURE - To result, to take effect.
IPSO FACTO - By the fact iself; by the mere fact.
ISSUE (n.) The disputed point or question in a case,

J

JEOPARDY - Danger, hazard, peril.
JOINDER - Joining; uniting with another person in some legal steps or proceeding.
JOINT - United; combined.
JUDGE - Member or members or representative or representatives of a court conducting a trial or hearing at which evidence is introduced.
JUDGMENT - The official decision of a court of justice.
JUDICIAL OR JUDICIARY - Relating to or connected with the administration of justice.
JURAT - The clause written at the foot of an affidavit, stating when, where and before whom such affidavit was sworn.
JURISDICTION - The authority to hear and determine controversies between parties.
JURISPRUDENCE - The philosophy of law.
JURY - A body of persons legally selected to inquire into any matter of fact, and to render their verdict according to the evidence.

L

LACHES - The failure to diligently assert a right, which results in a refusal to allow relief.

LANDLORD AND TENANT - A phrase used to denote the legal relation existing between the owner and occupant of real estate.
LARCENY - Stealing personal property belonging to another.
LATENT - Hidden; that which does not appear on the face of a thing.
LAW - Includes constitutional, statutory, and decisional law.
LAWYER-CLIENT PRIVILEGE - (1) A "client" is a person, public officer, or corporation, association, or other organization or entity, either public or private, who is rendered professional legal services by a lawyer, or who consults a lawyer with a view to obtaining professional legal services from him; (2) A "lawyer" is a person authorized, or reasonably believed by the client to be authorized, to practice law in any state or nation; (3) A "representative of the lawyer" is one employed to assist the lawyer in the rendition of professional legal services; (4) A communication is "confidential" if not intended to be disclosed to third persons other than those to whom disclosure is in furtherance of the rendition of professional legal services to the client or those reasonably necessary for the transmission of the communication.

General rule of privilege - A client has a privilege to refuse to disclose and to prevent any other person from disclosing confidential communications made for the purpose of facilitating the rendition of professional legal services to the client, (1) between himself or his representative and his lawyer or his lawyer's representative, or (2) between his lawyer and the lawyer's representative, or (3) by him or his lawyer to a lawyer representing another in a matter of common interest, or (4) between representatives of the client or between the client and a representative of the client, or (5) between lawyers representing the client.
LEADING QUESTION - Question that suggests to the witness the answer that the examining party desires.
LEASE - A contract by which one conveys real estate for a limited time usually for a specified rent; personal property also may be leased.
LEGISLATION - The act of enacting laws.
LEGITIMATE - Lawful.
LESSEE - One to whom a lease is given.
LESSOR - One who grants a lease
LEVY - A collecting or exacting by authority.
LIABLE - Responsible; bound or obligated in law or equity.
LIBEL (v.) - To defame or injure a person's reputation by a published writing.
 (n.) - The initial pleading on the part of the plaintiff in an admiralty proceeding.
LIEN - A hold or claim which one person has upon the property of another as a security for some debt or charge.
LIQUIDATED - Fixed; settled.
LIS PENDENS - A pending civil or criminal action.
LITERAL - According to the language.
LITIGANT - A party to a lawsuit.
LITATION - A judicial controversy.
LOCUS - A place.
LOCUS DELICTI - Place of the crime.
LOCUS POENITENTIAE - The abandoning or giving up of one's intention to commit some crime before it is fully completed or abandoning a conspiracy before its purpose is accomplished.

M

MALFEASANCE - To do a wrongful act.
MALICE - The doing of a wrongful act Intentionally without just cause or excuse.

MANDAMUS - The name of a writ issued by a court to enforce the performance of some public duty.
MANDATORY (adj.) Containing a command.
MARITIME - Pertaining to the sea or to commerce thereon.
MARSHALING - Arranging or disposing of in order.
MAXIM - An established principle or proposition.
MINISTERIAL - That which involves obedience to instruction, but demands no special discretion, judgment or skill.
MISAPPROPRIATE - Dealing fraudulently with property entrusted to one.
MISDEMEANOR - A crime less than a felony and punishable by a fine or imprisonment for less than one year.
MISFEASANCE - Improper performance of a lawful act.
MISREPRESENTATION - An untrue representation of facts.
MITIGATE - To make or become less severe, harsh.
MITTIMUS - A warrant of commitment to prison.
MOOT (adj.) Unsettled, undecided, not necessary to be decided.
MORTGAGE - A conveyance of property upon condition, as security for the payment of a debt or the performance of a duty, and to become void upon payment or performance according to the stipulated terms.
MORTGAGEE - A person to whom property is mortgaged.
MORTGAGOR - One who gives a mortgage.
MOTION - In legal proceedings, a "motion" is an application, either written or oral, addressed to the court by a party to an action or a suit requesting the ruling of the court on a matter of law.
MUTUALITY - Reciprocation.

N

NEGLIGENCE - The failure to exercise that degree of care which an ordinarily prudent person would exercise under like circumstances.
NEGOTIABLE (instrument) - Any instrument obligating the payment of money which is transferable from one person to another by endorsement and delivery or by delivery only.
NEGOTIATE - To transact business; to transfer a negotiable instrument; to seek agreement for the amicable disposition of a controversy or case.
NOLLE PROSEQUI - A formal entry upon the record, by the plaintiff in a civil suit or the prosecuting officer in a criminal action, by which he declares that he "will no further prosecute" the case.
NOLO CONTENDERE - The name of a plea in a criminal action, having the same effect as a plea of guilty; but not constituting a direct admission of guilt.
NOMINAL - Not real or substantial.
NOMINAL DAMAGES - Award of a trifling sum where no substantial injury is proved to have been sustained.
NONFEASANCE - Neglect of duty.
NOVATION - The substitution of a new debt or obligation for an existing one.
NUNC PRO TUNC - A phrase applied to acts allowed to be done after the time when they should be done, with a retroactive effect.("Now for then.")

O

OATH - Oath includes affirmation or declaration under penalty of perjury.
OBITER DICTUM - Opinion expressed by a court on a matter not essentially involved in a case and hence not a decision; also called dicta, if plural.

OBJECT (v.) - To oppose as improper or illegal and referring the question of its propriety or legality to the court.
OBLIGATION - A legal duty, by which a person is bound to do or not to do a certain thing.
OBLIGEE - The person to whom an obligation is owed.
OBLIGOR - The person who is to perform the obligation.
OFFER (v.) - To present for acceptance or rejection.
    (n.) - A proposal to do a thing, usually a proposal to make a contract.
OFFICIAL INFORMATION - Information within the custody or control of a department or agency of the government the disclosure of which is shown to be contrary to the public interest.
OFFSET - A deduction.
ONUS PROBANDI - Burden of proof.
OPINION - The statement by a judge of the decision reached in a case, giving the law as applied to the case and giving reasons for the judgment; also a belief or view.
OPTION - The exercise of the power of choice; also a privilege existing in one person, for which he has paid money, which gives him the right to buy or sell real or personal property at a given price within a specified time.
ORDER - A rule or regulation; every direction of a court or judge made or entered in writing but not including a judgment.
ORDINANCE - Generally, a rule established by authority; also commonly used to designate the legislative acts of a municipal corporation.
ORIGINAL - Writing or recording itself or any counterpart intended to have the same effect by a person executing or issuing it. An "original" of a photograph includes the negative or any print therefrom. If data are stored in a computer or similar device, any printout or other output readable by sight, shown to reflect the data accurately, is an "original."
OVERT - Open, manifest.

P

PANEL - A group of jurors selected to serve during a term of the court.
PARENS PATRIAE - Sovereign power of a state to protect or be a guardian over children and incompetents.
PAROL - Oral or verbal.
PAROLE - To release one in prison before the expiration of his sentence, conditionally.
PARITY - Equality in purchasing power between the farmer and other segments of the economy.
PARTITION - A legal division of real or personal property between one or more owners.
PARTNERSHIP - An association of two or more persons to carry on as co-owners a business for profit.
PATENT (adj.) - Evident.
    (n.) - A grant of some privilege, property, or authority, made by the government or sovereign of a country to one or more individuals.
PECULATION - Stealing.
PECUNIARY - Monetary.
PENULTIMATE - Next to the last.
PER CURIAM - A phrase used in the report of a decision to distinguish an opinion of the whole court from an opinion written by any one judge.
PER SE - In itself; taken alone.
PERCEIVE - To acquire knowledge through one's senses.
PEREMPTORY - Imperative; absolute.
PERJURY - To lie or state falsely under oath.

PERPETUITY - Perpetual existence; also the quality or condition of an estate limited so that it will not take effect or vest within the period fixed by law.
PERSON - Includes a natural person, firm, association, organization, partnership, business trust, corporation, or public entity.
PERSONAL PROPERTY - Includes money, goods, chattels, things in action, and evidences of debt.
PERSONALTY - Short term for personal property.
PETITION - An application in writing for an order of the court, stating the circumstances upon which it is founded and requesting any order or other relief from a court.
PLAINTIFF - A person who brings a court action.
PLEA - A pleading in a suit or action.
PLEADINGS - Formal allegations made by the parties of their respective claims and defenses, for the judgment of the court.
PLEDGE - A deposit of personal property as a security for the performance of an act.
PLEDGEE - The party to whom goods are delivered in pledge.
PLEDGOR - The party delivering goods in pledge.
PLENARY - Full; complete.
POLICE POWER - Inherent power of the state or its political subdivisions to enact laws within constitutional limits to promote the general welfare of society or the community.
POLLING THE JURY - Call the names of persons on a jury and requiring each juror to declare what his verdict is before it is legally recorded.
POST MORTEM - After death.
POWER OF ATTORNEY - A writing authorizing one to act for another.
PRECEPT - An order, warrant, or writ issued to an officer or body of officers, commanding him or them to do some act within the scope of his or their powers.
PRELIMINARY FACT - Fact upon the existence or nonexistence of which depends the admissibility or inadmissibility of evidence. The phrase "the admissibility or inadmissibility of evidence" includes the qualification or disqualification of a person to be a witness and the existence or nonexistence of a privilege.
PREPONDERANCE - Outweighing.
PRESENTMENT - A report by a grand jury on something they have investigated on their own knowledge.
PRESUMPTION - An assumption of fact resulting from a rule of law which requires such fact to be assumed from another fact or group of facts found or otherwise established in the action.
PRIMA FACUE - At first sight.
PRIMA FACIE CASE - A case where the evidence is very patent against the defendant.
PRINCIPAL - The source of authority or rights; a person primarily liable as differentiated from "principle" as a primary or basic doctrine.
PRO AND CON - For and against.
PRO RATA - Proportionally.
PROBATE - Relating to proof, especially to the proof of wills.
PROBATIVE - Tending to prove.
PROCEDURE - In law, this term generally denotes rules which are established by the Federal, State, or local Governments regarding the types of pleading and courtroom practice which must be followed by the parties involved in a criminal or civil case.
PROCLAMATION - A public notice by an official of some order, intended action, or state of facts.

PROFFERED EVIDENCE - The admissibility or inadmissibility of which is dependent upon the existence or nonexistence of a preliminary fact.
PROMISSORY (NOTE) - A promise in writing to pay a specified sum at an expressed time, or on demand, or at sight, to a named person, or to his order, or bearer.
PROOF - The establishment by evidence of a requisite degree of belief concerning a fact in the mind of the trier of fact or the court.
PROPERTY - Includes both real and personal property.
PROPRIETARY (adj.) - Relating or pertaining to ownership; usually a single owner.
PROSECUTE - To carry on an action or other judicial proceeding; to proceed against a person criminally.
PROVISO - A limitation or condition in a legal instrument.
PROXIMATE - Immediate; nearest
PUBLIC EMPLOYEE - An officer, agent, or employee of a public entity.
PUBLIC ENTITY - Includes a national, state, county, city and county, city, district, public authority, public agency, or any other political subdivision or public corporation, whether foreign or domestic.
PUBLIC OFFICIAL - Includes an official of a political dubdivision of such state or territory and of a municipality.
PUNITIVE - Relating to punishment.

Q

QUASH - To make void.
QUASI - As if; as it were.
QUID PRO QUO - Something for something; the giving of one valuable thing for another.
QUITCLAIM (v.) - To release or relinquish claim or title to, especially in deeds to realty.
QUO WARRANTO - A legal procedure to test an official's right to a public office or the right to hold a franchise, or to hold an office in a domestic corporation.

R

RATIFY - To approve and sanction.
REAL PROPERTY - Includes lands, tenements, and hereditaments.
REALTY - A brief term for real property.
REBUT - To contradict; to refute, especially by evidence and arguments.
RECEIVER - A person who is appointed by the court to receive, and hold in trust property in litigation.
RECIDIVIST - Habitual criminal.
RECIPROCAL - Mutual.
RECOUPMENT - To keep back or get something which is due; also, it is the right of a defendant to have a deduction from the amount of the plaintiff's damages because the plaintiff has not fulfilled his part of the same contract.
RECROSS EXAMINATION - Examination of a witness by a cross-examiner subsequent to a redirect examination of the witness.
REDEEM - To release an estate or article from mortgage or pledge by paying the debt for which it stood as security.
REDIRECT EXAMINATION - Examination of a witness by the direct examiner subsequent to the cross-examination of the witness.
REFEREE - A person to whom a cause pending in a court is referred by the court, to take testimony, hear the parties, and report thereon to the court.

REFERENDUM - A method of submitting an important legislative or administrative matter to a direct vote of the people.

RELEVANT EVIDENCE - Evidence including evidence relevant to the credulity of a witness or hearsay declarant, having any tendency in reason to prove or disprove any disputed fact that is of consequence to the determination of the action.

REMAND - To send a case back to the lower court from which it came, for further proceedings.

REPLEVIN - An action to recover goods or chattels wrongfully taken or detained.

REPLY (REPLICATION) - Generally, a reply is what the plaintiff or other person who has instituted proceedings says in answer to the defendant's case.

RE JUDICATA - A thing judicially acted upon or decided.

RES ADJUDICATA - Doctrine that an issue or dispute litigated and determined in a case between the opposing parties is deemed permanently decided between these parties.

RESCIND (RECISSION) - To avoid or cancel a contract.

RESPONDENT - A defendant in a proceeding in chancery or admiralty; also, the person who contends against the appeal in a case.

RESTITUTION - In equity, it is the restoration of both parties to their original condition (when practicable), upon the rescission of a contract for fraud or similar cause.

RETROACTIVE (RETROSPECTIVE) - Looking back; effective as of a prior time.

REVERSED - A term used by appellate courts to indicate that the decision of the lower court in the case before it has been set aside.

REVOKE - To recall or cancel.

RIPARIAN (RIGHTS) - The rights of a person owning land containing or bordering on a water course or other body of water, such as lakes and rivers.

S

SALE - A contract whereby the ownership of property is transferred from one person to another for a sum of money or for any consideration.

SANCTION - A penalty or punishment provided as a means of enforcing obedience to a law; also, an authorization.

SATISFACTION - The discharge of an obligation by paying a party what is due to him; or what is awarded to him by the judgment of a court or otherwise.

SCIENTER - Knowingly; also, it is used in pleading to denote the defendant's guilty knowledge.

SCINTILLA - A spark; also the least particle.

SECRET OF STATE - Governmental secret relating to the national defense or the international relations of the United States.

SECURITY - Indemnification; the term is applied to an obligation, such as a mortgage or deed of trust, given by a debtor to insure the payment or performance of his debt, by furnishing the creditor with a resource to be used in case of the debtor's failure to fulfill the principal obligation.

SENTENCE - The judgment formally pronounced by the court or judge upon the defendant after his conviction in a criminal prosecution.

SET-OFF - A claim or demand which one party in an action credits against the claim of the opposing party.

SHALL and MAY - "Shall" is mandatory and "may" is permissive.

SITUS - Location.

SOVEREIGN - A person, body or state in which independent and supreme authority is vested.

STARE DECISIS - To follow decided cases.

STATE - "State" means this State, unless applied to the different parts of the United States. In the latter case, it includes any state, district, commonwealth, territory or insular possession of the United States, including the District of Columbia.

STATEMENT - (a) Oral or written verbal expression or (b) nonverbal conduct of a person intended by him as a substitute for oral or written verbal expression.

STATUTE - An act of the legislature. Includes a treaty.

STATUTE OF LIMITATION - A statute limiting the time to bring an action after the right of action has arisen.

STAY - To hold in abeyance an order of a court.

STIPULATION - Any agreement made by opposing attorneys regulating any matter incidental to the proceedings or trial.

SUBORDINATION (AGREEMENT) - An agreement making one's rights inferior to or of a lower rank than another's.

SUBORNATION - The crime of procuring a person to lie or to make false statements to a court.

SUBPOENA - A writ or order directed to a person, and requiring his attendance at a particular time and place to testify as a witness.

SUBPOENA DUCES TECUM - A subpoena used, not only for the purpose of compelling witnesses to attend in court, but also requiring them to bring with them books or documents which may be in their possession, and which may tend to elucidate the subject matter of the trial.

SUBROGATION - The substituting of one for another as a creditor, the new creditor succeeding to the former's rights.

SUBSIDY - A government grant to assist a private enterprise deemed advantageous to the public.

SUI GENERIS - Of the same kind.

SUIT - Any civil proceeding by a person or persons against another or others in a court of justice by which the plaintiff pursues the remedies afforded him by law.

SUMMONS - A notice to a defendant that an action against him has been commenced and requiring him to appear in court and answer the complaint.

SUPRA - Above; this word occurring by itself in a book refers the reader to a previous part of the book.

SURETY - A person who binds himself for the payment of a sum of money, or for the performance of something else, for another.

SURPLUSAGE - Extraneous or unnecessary matter.

SURVIVORSHIP - A term used when a person becomes entitled to property by reason of his having survived another person who had an interest in the property.

SUSPEND SENTENCE - Hold back a sentence pending good behavior of prisoner.

SYLLABUS - A note prefixed to a report, especially a case, giving a brief statement of the court's ruling on different issues of the case.

T

TALESMAN - Person summoned to fill a panel of jurors.

TENANT - One who holds or possesses lands by any kind of right or title; also, one who has the temporary use and occupation of real property owned by another person (landlord), the duration and terms of his tenancy being usually fixed by an instrument called "a lease."

TENDER - An offer of money; an expression of willingness to perform a contract according to its terms.

TERM - When used with reference to a court, it signifies the period of time during which the court holds a session, usually of several weeks or months duration.

TESTAMENTARY - Pertaining to a will or the administration of a will.
TESTATOR (male)
TESTATRIX (female) - One who makes or has made a testament or will.
TESTIFY (TESTIMONY) - To give evidence under oath as a witness.
TO WIT - That is to say; namely.
TORT - Wrong; injury to the person.
TRANSITORY - Passing from place to place.
TRESPASS - Entry into another's ground, illegally.
TRIAL - The examination of a cause, civil or criminal, before a judge who has jurisdiction over it, according to the laws of the land.
TRIER OF FACT - Includes (a) the jury and (b) the court when the court is trying an issue of fact other than one relating to the admissibility of evidence.
TRUST - A right of property, real or personal, held by one party for the benefit of another.
TRUSTEE - One who lawfully holds property in custody for the benefit of another.

U

UNAVAILABLE AS A WITNESS - The declarant is (1) Exempted or precluded on the ground of privilege from testifying concerning the matter to which his statement is relevant; (2) Disqualified from testifying to the matter; (3) Dead or unable to attend or to testify at the hearing because of then existing physical or mental illness or infirmity; (4) Absent from the hearing and the court is unable to compel his attendance by its process; or (5) Absent from the hearing and the proponent of his statement has exercised reasonable diligence but has been unable to procure his attendance by the court's process.
ULTRA VIRES - Acts beyond the scope and power of a corporation, association, etc.
UNILATERAL - One-sided; obligation upon, or act of one party.
USURY - Unlawful interest on a loan.

V

VACATE - To set aside; to move out.
VARIANCE - A discrepancy or disagreement between two instruments or two aspects of the same case, which by law should be consistent.
VENDEE - A purchaser or buyer.
VENDOR - The person who transfers property by sale, particularly real estate; the term "seller" is used more commonly for one who sells personal property.
VENIREMEN - Persons ordered to appear to serve on a jury or composing a panel of jurors.
VENUE - The place at which an action is tried, generally based on locality or judicial district in which an injury occurred or a material fact happened.
VERDICT - The formal decision or finding of a jury.
VERIFY - To confirm or substantiate by oath.
VEST - To accrue to.
VOID - Having no legal force or binding effect.
VOIR DIRE - Preliminary examination of a witness or a juror to test competence, interest, prejudice, etc.

W

WAIVE - To give up a right.
WAIVER - The intentional or voluntary relinquishment of a known right.
WARRANT (WARRANTY) (v.) - To promise that a certain fact or state of facts, in relation to the subject matter, is, or shall be, as it is represented to be.

WARRANT (n.) - A writ issued by a judge, or other competent authority, addressed to a sheriff, or other officer, requiring him to arrest the person therein named, and bring him before the judge or court to answer or be examined regarding the offense with which he is charged.

WRIT - An order or process issued in the name of the sovereign or in the name of a court or judicial officer, commanding the performance or nonperformance of some act.

WRITING - Handwriting, typewriting, printing, photostating, photographing and every other means of recording upon any tangible thing any form of communication or representation, including letters, words, pictures, sounds, or symbols, or combinations thereof.

WRITINGS AND RECORDINGS - Consists of letters, words, or numbers, or their equivalent, set down by handwriting, typewriting, printing, photostating, photographing, magnetic impulse, mechanical or electronic recording, or other form of data compilation.

Y

YEA AND NAY - Yes and no.

YELLOW DOG CONTRACT - A contract by which employer requires employee to sign an instrument promising as condition that he will not join a union during its continuance, and will be discharged if he does join.

Z

ZONING - The division of a city by legislative regulation into districts and the prescription and application in each district of regulations having to do with structural and architectural designs of buildings and of regulations prescribing use to which buildings within designated districts may be put.

www.ingramcontent.com/pod-product-compliance
Lightning Source LLC
Chambersburg PA
CBHW082046300426
44117CB00015B/2630